ABRACADABRA!

ABRACADABRA!

FUN MAGIC TRICKS FOR KIDS

KRISTEN KELLY & KEN KELLY

PHOTOGRAPHS BY COLETTE KELLY
FOREWORD BY JULIAN MATHER

Sky Pony Press
New York

Visit our website at skyponypress.com.

10 9 8 7 6 5 4 3 2 1

Library of Congress Cataloging-in-Publication Data is available on file.

Cover design by Sarah Brody
Cover photograph by Colette Kelly

Print ISBN: 978-1-5107-0296-7
Ebook ISBN: 978-1-5107-0297-4

Printed in China

Contents ★

Foreword ★

Read this aloud to yourself. Really, no kiddin'. Go on:

> Knock, knock.
> Who's there?
> I'm a pile up.
> I'm a pile up, who?
> So you're a pile of poo, huh!

If you laughed at this then you get my sense of humor.

Ken Kelly and Kristen Kelly laughed at this. That's how I knew we could work together teaching magic tricks to kids.

My name is Julian Mather and I live in Australia. I teach magic on YouTube. Little did I know that on the other side of the world in England, twenty-three hours away by plane, Ken and Kristen were teaching magic online, too.

One day, Ken sent me an email. And here's the thing—I almost didn't open it because I was too busy trying to find someone I trusted to team up with to teach magic tricks. Am I glad I opened that email! We quickly realized we like teaching the same sort of magic.

That's fun magic, that's entertaining magic, that's magic that makes people smile.

If you like that sort of magic, then this book will delight you.

I know great magic teachers when I see them. Ken and Kristen are the *best* around. Consider yourself one of the lucky ones if you are reading this now.

REMEMBER THIS:

With every trick you learn here, you need to add one extra little thing to your performance: a smile.

Smiling will take your tricks to the next level.

Get ready . . . but first, read this poem before you start learning your first magic trick:

> Smiling is infectious,
> You can catch it like the flu.
> Someone smiled at me today,
> And I started smiling too.

—Julian Mather

Introduction ★

THE REAL SECRET OF MAGICIANS

The book you hold in your hands right now contains the biggest magic secret of all.

If you are just discovering magic, then welcome! This book can change your life if you want it to. If you already do magic, then you are going to love the magic tricks you find in *Abracadabra!*.

My name is Ken Kelly and I have been a professional magician for more than thirty years, making a living from the magic shows I perform. Writing this book has been a family project with Kristen, my daughter, who helped with the tricks, and Colette, Kristen's mum, who took all the pictures.

The illusions within these pages are not just silly tricks for kids. They are routines I have performed as a working magician. You will be learning magic tricks that will astonish your audience and, with a little practice, you will look like a superstar magician.

All the magic tricks come with step-by-step instructions on how to make and perform the magic with nice photographs to make learning easy. Every trick has its own video that you can watch if you have access to the Internet. Either use the QR code with a smartphone or go to the web address and you will be taken to a video performance and explanation for each trick.

Before I tell you the biggest magic secret of all, let me tell you why I wrote this book for you.

I received a magic set when I was six years old. I remember showing my grandmother a trick that I had learned from the set and she was totally amazed. She wanted to know how I did it.

I didn't tell, because the first rule of magic is that a magician never reveals their secrets to the audience. I remember feeling rather special about that first trick because I realized that I could do something that other people couldn't.

I decided right there and then that I wanted to learn more magic, and I went to my local library to get books about magic. The more I learned about magic, the more my love for magic grew, and the more I performed. I found that magic gave me confidence—I was able to stand in front of large groups and speak with ease. At school everyone knew me as the magic man.

When Kristen, my daughter, turned six years old, she decided she wanted to learn magic too, so I started looking around for good magic books for children. I found it difficult to find a good book all about magic tricks for kids, so Kristen and I decided to write our own. We hope you like it.

THE BIGGEST MAGIC SECRET OF ALL:

When you see magic and you don't know how it works, it fills you with wonder and excitement. When you start learning how to do magic it can sometimes be a bit of a letdown when you learn how a trick is done. A magic trick that looked so amazing can suddenly become quite obvious once you know the secret.

Many people think that magic is about learning secrets. It's not. Anyone can learn secrets; that's easy. The true secret of magic is being able to perform the magic trick for someone else. The true secret of magic is creating that wonder and amazement in others. For magic to be magic, there must be someone to perform it—and that's where you come in.

By reading this book, you are taking on the responsibility to learn the tricks and practice them so you can perform them well in front of an audience. There is a saying that there are three rules of magic: practice, practice, and practice. This is not true. The real three rules of magic are practice, practice, and *perform*, because without the performance, there is no magic.

The true secret of magic is *you*, because without you doing the magic, this book simply becomes a list of secrets and that's of no use to anyone.

By sharing your magic, you will be giving a gift to others. That's real magic.

In turn, I am only able to share with you the gift of magic in this book because of the people who have given to me.

Paul Málek, my magic teacher, shared his knowledge and wisdom with me over many decades. I am the magician I am today thanks to Paul. If it were not for him, I wouldn't be a magician and this book would never have been written.

Julian Mather from Julian's Magician School on YouTube is a magician in Brisbane, Australia. Julian selflessly passed this book opportunity to Kristen and me to write. Without Julian sharing this opportunity, there would be no book in your hand now.

Pat Flynn from smartpassiveincome.com is not a magician, but he loves magic and performs from time to time. Pat willingly shared his time and knowledge to help me create MagicTricksForKids.org, which in turn led to this book being written. Without Pat, this book would never have been.

There are many others who have given and shared with me and made this book possible. To all of them, I say thank you.

Let's get on to learning some magic tricks that you can make and do!

—Ken Kelly

ABRACADABRA!

How to Watch ★

Each and every magic trick in this book comes with its own video that shows you how to perform the illusion. If you want to watch the videos, you will need to go on the Internet using a smartphone, tablet, laptop, or computer. It's best to ask an adult for permission and help with this.

On the first page of every trick in this book, there is a special website link and QR code that you can use to watch the video performance by Ken and Kristen Kelly.

A QR code looks like a square-shaped squiggle of patterns. To make a QR code work, you need a smartphone or tablet that is connected to the Internet. You will also need to download a QR code reader app. QR code reader apps are free and you can find them on the app store that supports your mobile or tablet. Once the QR code reader app has been installed, you can use your mobile or tablet camera to scan the QR code on the page, and you will be taken directly to the website with the video.

This book has been written in such a way that you do not need the video to be able to learn the tricks, so don't worry if you're unable to watch the video; you're not missing anything.

Anti-Gravity Coin ★

Money and magic go hand-in-hand. Since you're a magician, you don't have just regular coins in your piggy bank—you have *magic* coins! In the Anti-Gravity Coin magic trick, you'll learn exactly how to put your magic coins to work and wow the crowd.

Here's a fun and helpful video tutorial for the Anti-Gravity Coin trick using this QR code. Or, visit the website: http://magictricksforkids.org/agc/

EFFECT (WHAT THE AUDIENCE SEES):

You have one coin hidden in each hand, and one coin balanced on each of your closed fists (that means each hand has two coins).

Next, you try to catch the coins as they fall from the top of your fingers, but you "mess up" and both coins fall on the table. You ask an audience member to replace the coins back on your hand. However, magically and invisibly, you reveal that one coin has miraculously traveled from one hand to your other hand, where you now have three coins instead of two! Now, everyone will be wondering how you made that extra coin move from one hand to the other. Your answer? Magic!

YOU WILL NEED:

- 4 coins of the same size—about 1 inch in diameter
- A **close-up** magician's mat or soft surface (a folded blanket will work as well)

Tips:

In this anti-gravity coin magic trick we used American dollars. British 50 pence coins work well or any coin with a diameter of about 1 inch.

A **close-up** mat is a high density sponge that is about 5 mm thick and covered with a nonslip surface. It helps with the handling of the coins. It also absorbs sound and shocks so you won't have coins jumping off the table.

Close-up mats are easy to find on the Internet. Ask a parent to help you find it online.

You can also use a folded blanket or any similar soft surface to start with.

HOW THE TRICK IS PERFORMED:

STEP 2

Close your hands over the coins as shown in the picture. Hold your closed fists palms up.

Step 1

All you need is four shiny coins of the same value; if you have big coins, that's even better. Show your audience the four coins.

Your starting position: palms facing upwards, place one coin in the palm of each hand. Leave the other two coins on the mat.

STEP 3

Ask someone in your audience to place the two other coins on the mat on top of your fingers as shown in the picture—one coin balanced on top of each of your closed upturned fists.

You now have one coin in each hand already, and one coin balanced on top of each of your closed fists. Thank your audience member and ask them to take a seat.

STEP 4

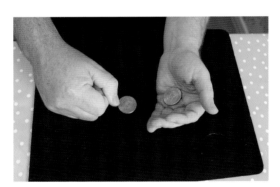

Sneaky move: In a swift move, turn both your hands over so that the backs of your closed fists are now facing upwards. While doing this, pretend that you're trying to catch the coins as they fall from the top of your fists, but instead let two coins from your **left hand** fall to the table while you quickly catch the other coin that was on top of your **right hand** in your right palm. The audience thinks that you have messed up and dropped the two coins that were on top of your fists, but in fact you now have two coins in your right hand and none in the left. This takes a bit of practice to get right.

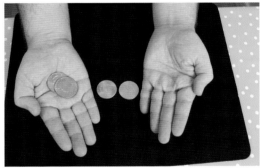

STEP 5

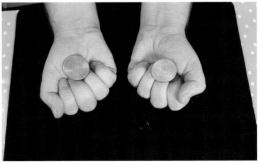

Pretend that you messed up. Ask your assistant from the audience to place the two coins back on top of your closed fingers so you can try again.

STEP 6

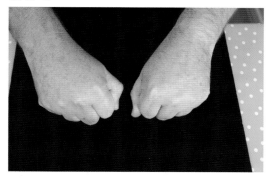

Quickly turn your hands over again, this time successfully catching the coins that fall from the top of your fingers.

STEP 7

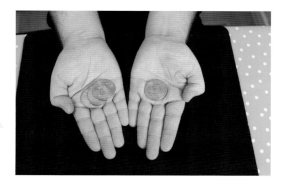

Moment of magic:
After a few seconds, open your left hand, revealing to the audience that one coin has disappeared. Now, slowly open the right hand and show that you have three coins there—the missing coin has "jumped across" as if by magic!

Bow as your audience applauds.

Well done!
You have made a coin magically jump from one hand to the other!

Enjoy this really cool anti-gravity coin magic trick.

Anti-Gravity Glass ★

Have you ever tried to make a house of cards just to have it fall down flat? You won't have to worry about spending hours making one now, when you can amaze your audience even more with the Anti-Gravity Glass magic trick! This is a trick that requires a deck of cards.

See the Anti-Gravity Glass trick performed in this video tutorial using this QR code.
Or, visit the website: http://magictricksforkids.org/agg/

EFFECT (WHAT THE AUDIENCE SEES):

You—the magician—shuffle a deck of cards and ask an audience member to stop the shuffling and choose the top card from the deck. After showing the audience your card, you stand the card upright on a table and it will not fall!

If that were not enough, take a cup that is filled with water and place the cup on top of the thin card that is standing upright. Amazing! Your audience will be enchanted after seeing you magically balance the cup on top of the card and will wonder how you did it. . . .

YOU WILL NEED:

- Couple of playing cards
- Scissors
- See-through sticky tape
- Glass or plastic cup that is filled with some water

MAKING THE TRICK:

STEP 1

Cut one of the cards in half across the length of the card.

STEP 2

Stick a length of see-through sticky tape along the cut edge of one of the halved cards.

STEP 3

Stick this halved card onto the back of the full playing card. You will now have a "flap," as shown in the pictures. Stick some tape on the other side of the halved card to secure it.

STEP 4

You have made your **"gimmick,"** or trick card, for the anti-gravity glass! When opened, the card will look like an upside-down T-shape. However, make sure you only show the side without the flap to your audience so they won't see anything.

Well done!

Now you have your **"gimmick"** for the anti-gravity glass magic trick.

This trick is so easy to do. Work on a good presentation—the story you tell while performing your trick will turn a good trick into a GREAT trick!

HOW THE TRICK IS PERFORMED:

STEP 1

Place the special card that you made with a flap—your **gimmick**—at the top of your deck of cards. This is the card that will help you balance the cup. Keep this special card at the top of your deck as you shuffle, so it will always be at the same place on the top. You will need to practice to get it right.

Shuffle a deck of cards in front of an audience. Ask an audience member to help you with your magic performance by telling you when to stop shuffling. Next, ask the audience member to point to the top card of the deck—this will be the special card.

Tell the audience member to sit down and watch the magic show with the others.

STEP 2

Show the flat side of the special card to the audience; be careful not to show the side with the flap!

Next, set the card on the table. As you do this, quickly and discreetly open the flap so that when you place the card on the table, it will stand upright without falling.

STEP 3

Moment of magic:
Take your magician's cup that has been filled with some water. Put on a show by taking a sip to demonstrate that it is real water! Then, gently place the cup right on top of the card that is standing upright. The position is the most important—you want to place the cup on top of the area where the flap connects with the main card. That's how you'll get a good balance.

As you put the cup on the card, act as if you're straining to find the right balance. Let go of your hand slowly, pretending as if you're ready to catch the cup if it falls over.

Once the cup is stable, your audience will be surprised that you could balance a heavy cup of water on top of a thin, light card! They will believe that you're a true magician!

Tips:
This is such an easy magic trick, and it is even easier to make; however, it has one of the coolest effects. When doing this trick, you will be relying on good angles. You also need to be careful about not flashing your gimmick, so make sure you practice this before performing in front of an audience.

Anti-Gravity Ring ★

In the Rubber Band and Ring magic trick (page 99), a ring moves up a rubber band string. The Anti-Gravity Ring is a fantastic follow-up trick. This magic trick shows you how you can do the impossible with your superstar magic skills—learn to make a ring move up an angled pen with your powerful mind!

Simple yet mind-blowing magic tricks like this are easy to learn, and you will be noticed as an outstanding magician.

See the demonstration for the Anti-Gravity Ring trick in this video tutorial using this QR code. Or, visit the website: http://magictricksforkids.org/agr/

EFFECT (WHAT THE AUDIENCE SEES):

You ask a lady from the audience if you can use her ring. If it's a diamond ring, even better! You place the ring on the end of a simple pen and tilt the pen at an angle.

As you wave your hands over the pen performing your magic, the ring slowly travels up the slope of the pen as if powered by your mind, even defying gravity! Your audience's eyes are glued to the moving ring and you've amazed them—not only are you a powerful and talented magician, but you've also just showed gravity who's the real boss!

YOU WILL NEED:

- Ball point pen with a removable ink chamber
- Lady's ring (from the audience)
- Invisible thread (see step 1)
- Safety pin
- See-through sticky tape
- Scissors

MAKING THE TRICK:

STEP 1

The secret of how to perform the anti-gravity ring magic trick is by using invisible thread.

You can buy invisible thread by simply searching the term "invisible thread" online. There are loads of places to get it from.

Or, you can learn to make your own invisible thread by visiting m.wikihow.com/Make-Invisible-Thread.

You will need to be a bit patient when working with invisible thread. It is very hard to see since it is so fine (but that is exactly what you want, remember!)

> The key to the Anti-Gravity Ring magic trick is a very thin filament or string. This string is so tiny that it's almost invisible, so your audience members don't see it.

STEP 2

To make the "**gimmick**" of the anti-gravity ring magic trick, you will need a pen and your invisible thread (for the purpose of these instructions, I have used visible black cotton thread so you can see what to do with your invisible thread).

Remove the ink chamber (also called the "reservoir") from the ballpoint pen's plastic tube. Fasten and wind one end of a piece of invisible thread around the tip of the pen, as shown in the picture.

Measure out the thread—it has to be long enough to extend from your chest to your hand as you hold the pen outstretched in front of you (about an arm's length).

STEP 3

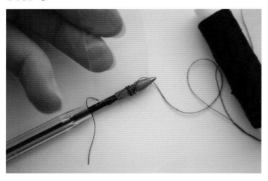

Secure the thread around the tip of the pen with a small piece of see-through sticky tape. The less you use the better as too much tape will make it difficult for the ink chamber to slide back inside the plastic tube. The pen needs to look un-gimmicked and natural. Push the ink chamber back into the tube, now with the invisible thread tied around it.

STEP 4

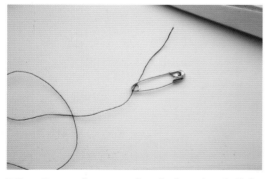

Tie the other end of the invisible thread to a safety pin. Be patient with this step—this is a simple magic trick to perform, but it takes time to set up.

Using the pin, attach the thread to your clothing, preferably under your waistband. Make sure that the

pin is out of sight from the audience. You are nearly ready to perform the anti-gravity ring magic trick!

HOW THE TRICK IS PERFORMED:

STEP 1

Before the performance: Make sure the safety pin is already attached under your waistband, hidden from view. The thread now runs from the safety pin under your clothes to the pen that you're holding out in front of you. With your fingers, hold the pen at the top end, with the pen nib pointing slightly upward. Hold it away from your body to create some tension on the thread.

STEP 2

In front of an audience, place the ring over the tip of the pen so it slides down to the end, resting on your fingers and catching the invisible thread along with it so that the thread now runs through the ring. Be careful with your movements as the thread might snap if it gets caught by accident.

STEP 3

Slowly pull the pen away. The ring will begin to move on its own at a slow pace! You can also just tilt the pen back and forth while the ring moves toward the end of the pen.

As you make the ring move, wave your hand and wiggle your fingers over the pen and ring to show off your magical hands—it'll add a magical touch to the whole performance.

STEP 4

After you've performed the trick, take your bow and give the ring back to the lady you borrowed it from. Your audience will watch your trick with such intensity that, once it is over, they'll be even more amazed by your magical mind!

Well done!

You have made and performed the Anti-Gravity Ring magic trick!

Simple magic tricks like this are easy and fun to learn and make.

Tips:

Once you've mastered the technique of making the ring move (seemingly with the powers of your mind), work on your presentation. This mystical magic trick is enhanced with a really good performance.

Color-Changing Card ★

Have you ever wondered how a chameleon can change its colors to blend in with its surroundings and hide from people or animals that are chasing it? Well, you'll find out with the Color-Changing Card magic trick! You'll show your audience that you're a unique chameleon magician who can change the colors of a card with a snap of your magical fingers.

> See the Color-Changing Card trick in action using this QR code.
> Or, visit the website: http://magictricksforkids.org/ccc/

EFFECT (WHAT THE AUDIENCE SEES):

You ask an audience member to choose a card from a deck of blue cards. Then, you split the deck in half and ask them to return the card they selected face-down to your deck without showing you what it is. When you fan out the deck on the table, a single red card appears among the blue cards. You turn the red card over and show the audience that it's the exact card that your assistant picked out! Everyone will be stunned and mystified by your skills. But the magic hasn't ended yet.

Next, you gather half of the deck in your hands and place the selected card face-up on top of that deck. As you wave your magic wand over the card, you remove it from the deck and rub it's back side against the other cards that are fanned out on your table. When you flip over the card, it has suddenly turned blue! How did the red card turn back to blue? Your audience will be wondering the same thing, and the secret of this magic trick will be revealed over the next few pages . . .

YOU WILL NEED:

- Pack of cards
- A card that has a different colored back (for example, if you have a blue pack of cards, you can use a single red card)
- Magician's wax

Tips:
To do this trick you need something called "**magician's wax.**" You can get this wax from magic shops or from online shops by searching on the Internet for "magician's wax." 100 percent beeswax will also work for this trick.

MAKING THE TRICK:

STEP 1

You are going to need a "secret" item—a "**double-backed card.**" The double-backed card has a blue back on one side and a red back on the other.

To make a double-backed card, stick two cards with different colored backs together using magician's wax. Stick the front of the cards together so that the different colored backs are facing outward and can be seen on each side.

STEP 2

Take a tiny piece of magician's wax and form a small ball. Stick it on the blue back of the double-backed card.

STEP 3

Place the double-backed card at the bottom of the pack of cards, with the different, opposite color (in this example, red) facing upward. The blue side with the wax stuck on it should be facing down. The piece of wax is now at the bottom of the pack of cards.

HOW THE TRICK IS PERFORMED:

STEP 1

Fan out your deck of cards (with the double-backed card and wax right

at the bottom). Ask an audience member to select a card from the deck.

> ### *Tip:*
> Be careful not to fan the deck out all the way to reveal the red card—you don't want your audience to see it! Just fan out the deck to show most of the cards.

STEP 2

Tell the audience member to look at the card without showing it to you. Once your assistant chooses a card, split your deck in half to form two piles. Hold the bottom pile, the one with the double-backed card, in your hand. Leave the other pile on the table.

STEP 3

Ask the audience member to return the selected card face-down on top of the pile on the table. Now, place the pile that has the double-backed card and wax right on top of the pile on the table, so that the double-backed card is on top of the audience member's selected card.

Secretly give the deck a gentle downward push to stick the double-backed card onto the selected card.

STEP 4

Spread the cards out on the table to reveal that one card has "changed color" to red. Pull out the red card and reveal to the audience that it's the card your assistant selected!

STEP 5

For the final effect, gather half the cards on one side of the double-backed card in your hands. Place the double-backed card, which is still stuck to the selected card, with the numbered side facing upward on top of the deck.

Moment of magic: With your fingers, smoothly and carefully remove the selected card from the double-backed card by twisting it gently, and it will unstick from the double-backed card.

STEP 6

For a magical effect, rub the card, numbered side facing upward, on the cards that are still fanned out on the table; you can even use a magic wand. Then, finish with a flourish, turning the selected card over to reveal that the back has changed color once again from red back to blue!

Fan out the other deck in your hand on the table, and there won't be a red card in sight! You're now known as the chameleon magician who can change the colors of a card with your superstar magic talent.

Well done!

You have performed the Color-Changing Card magic trick. This magic trick will astound your spectators and show off your skills as a true magician. Enjoy entertaining and mesmerizing your audiences.

Cup Through Table ★

Making objects go through tables? Only a magician can do that. You're a magician, so you can do the Cup Through Table magic trick, too! This fun trick can be done anywhere if you have a cup, paper, and a small object such as a ball or coin. It's one that will leave your guests thinking, "How did that amazing magician do it?" for hours after the show has ended.

Check out the video for the Cup Through Table magic trick using this QR code.
Or, visit the website: http://magictricksforkids.org/ctt/

EFFECT (WHAT THE AUDIENCE SEES):

You show your audience a magic ball, a magic cup, and a magic mystery "cloak." Tell your audience a story about your special ball and how you will make it go through the table magically.

You place the magic cup over the ball and wrap the "cloak" around the magic cup. This is so that the magic ball's secret doesn't get out too easily! Then, with a smash of your hand, you make the cup go through the table and leave the magic ball behind.

Although the ball didn't go through the table like you said, the cup went through instead. This "accidental" magic trick is even more marvelous and your audience will admire your skills.

YOU WILL NEED:

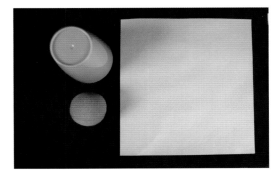

- Cup or glass
- Sponge ball or crumpled paper ball (that can fit under the cup or glass)
- Sheet of paper (letter or A4 size)
- Scissors

MAKING THE TRICK:

STEP 1

Start with a letter- or A4-sized piece of paper. We need to make a square out of it.

> *Tip:*
> Make sure that the paper you use covers the whole cup when wrapped over it. Refer to the video instructions to see what is meant by this.

STEP 2

Fold the top corner of the paper towards the lower opposite side. Fold it down to where the paper forms a right-angled triangle. Make sure all the corners touch each other. Flatten the side of the fold with your fingers.

STEP 3

Cut the rectangular piece off and open up the square.

> *Well done!*
> You have made a square piece of paper to perform the trick!
> The Cup Through Table magic trick works on the magic principle of misdirection. No gimmicks are required and it is all about the presentation.

HOW THE TRICK IS PERFORMED:

STEP 1

This magic trick should be performed on top of a solid, covered table. You can use a ball, a coin, or anything that will fit under the cup. Show your audience that your table is solid by knocking on the table.

STEP 2

Tell your audience that you'll be making the ball go through the table, but you're actually going to make the *cup* go through it. This is called **misdirection**, where you direct the audience's attention on one object to take their focus off another object. This is a popular magician's technique since it makes the magic trick much more exciting.

Tell your audience that you need a magic "cloak," which is the square piece of paper, to wrap around the cup. This is a special cloak that will help your magic ball go through the table. You can also share some other story to make the magic trick performance more interesting for your crowd.

STEP 3

Place your cup over the ball. Wrap the paper around the cup. Then, remove the cup and paper and release the cup into your lap quickly and secretly. Make sure your audience can't see the cup dropping in your lap.

Next, place the paper, which has kept the shape of the cup, over the ball. Holding the paper with one hand, quickly smash your other hand down on the paper, squishing it flat on the table.

STEP 4

Remove the paper and reveal that the cup is gone though the ball is still there! Reach down from under the table and show your audience the cup that went through the table.

Even though you didn't make the ball go through the table, you made the cup go through, and that's even more incredible magic. Your audience will love it!

Cutting a Lady in Half ★

"How do you do that?!" is the most common audience reaction when they see a magician cut someone in half at a magic show—and the person isn't hurt at all! What you may not know is that you can do this same famous magic trick, too. It's insanely easy to perform, and you'll be an even more popular magician after you've shocked your audience with your advanced magic skills.

Cutting a lady in half might sound dangerous and evil, but magicians are always all about fun. This trick is completely safe and kid-friendly to perform! You won't be pinned as a criminal even after you've revealed it to your audience.

Watch how the Cutting a Lady in Half magic trick is performed in this video tutorial using this QR code. Or, visit this website: http://magictricksforkids.org/calih/

EFFECT (WHAT THE AUDIENCE SEES):

You have two sheets of paper: one is a magic wooden box and the other is a lady. The audience will see you slip the lady inside the box, with her head and feet poking out from either side. Two "doors" in the magic box open up to reveal the lady's body inside.

In front of the audience's eyes, you cut the magic box, with the lady inside, in half. Then, you'll take the lady out of the cut magic box, revealing that her body is still intact! You're now just like the famous magicians and illusionists who perform this trick on stage.

YOU WILL NEED:

- Scissors
- Glue stick
- Masking tape
- Beads, buttons, or stickers for the "handles"
- The "bamboo effect" printout (pg 28)
- The "magic box" printout (pg 29)
- The "lady" printout (pg 30)

Tips:

Print out all the graphic elements before you start.

It works best if you print the "magic box" graphic on cardboard. If you can't print on cardboard, glue the printout to an A4- or letter-sized sheet of cardboard. Using cardboard gives the box a little more stiffness than just using paper.

Ask a grown-up for help with cutting the "doors" and slits in your magic box printout.

MAKING THE TRICK:

STEP 1

Cut along the solid black line that makes the outline of the magic box graphic (hint: look for the scissors symbol).

STEP 2

Cut the two slits in the back of the magic box as shown.

STEP 3

Now cut out the bamboo effect. This will be the front of your magic box.

STEP 4

Cover the back of the bamboo effect paper with glue. It needs to stick down flat without any bubbles. Glue it to the non-printed side of the magic box paper. Make sure that it matches up with the front of the box (where the two rectangular "doors" are) on the reverse side; don't stick it over the slits you've cut in **Step 3**.

STEP 5

Trim off the bamboo effect paper that is sticking over the edge of the box, as shown in the picture.

STEP 6

Now it is time to cut the "doors" in your box. Cut along the solid black lines to make two flaps. *Do not* cut the doors off. Fold the doors at the dotted lines.

STEP 7

Fold your magic box along the dotted line that is running across the middle of the graphic. You are only a few steps away from completing your magic box to perform the Cutting a Lady in Half magic trick.

STEP 8

Using masking tape, stick the bottom front edge to the bottom back edge. You now have a sleeve. Stick masking tape over the folded edge too to make it look the same as the bottom edge.

STEP 9

Glue a couple of buttons or beads on the doors of the magic box for extra effect. You can also use stickers or draw handles on as you wish.

STEP 10

Fold the "lady" graphic in half along the long edge.

STEP 11

Spread the inside with glue and press the sides together to stick.

STEP 12

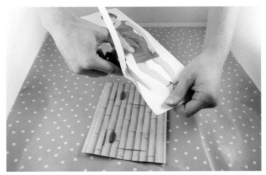

Trim the edge off along the dotted line.

> *Almost there!*
> You have your **gimmick** for the Cutting the Lady in Half magic trick.
>   Ready for the handling?

HOW THE TRICK IS PERFORMED:

STEP 1

Slide your lady into the side of the magic box. Her head and feet should stick out from either sides. Open the "doors" in the magic box to show the audience her body that is inside the box.

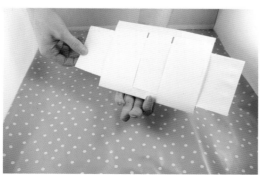

However, what the audience doesn't see is that the lady weaves through the slits in the back of the magic box, as shown in the picture.

STEP 2

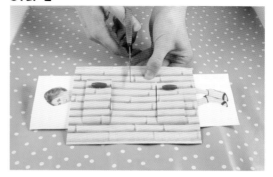

In front of your audience, get ready to cut the lady in half with a pair of scissors. Hold the front of the box up toward your audience so they don't see the back of the box.

Moment of magic: As you cut, your scissors should avoid the lady, as shown in the picture, and only cut through the magic box. However, the audience only sees the front of the box and the lady being cut in half!

Tips:
The trick to the Cutting a Lady in Half performance is the extra sheet of paper behind the front of the magic box. This sheet has slits in it, and it allows you to weave the lady through it. The sheet protects the lady. See? You won't hurt anyone in this magic trick!

STEP 3

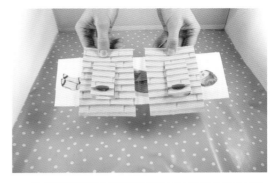

With a flourish, slowly remove the magic box that is cut in half and show the audience that the lady is still whole!

Well done!
Ta-Da! You have completed the Cutting a Lady in Half illusion!

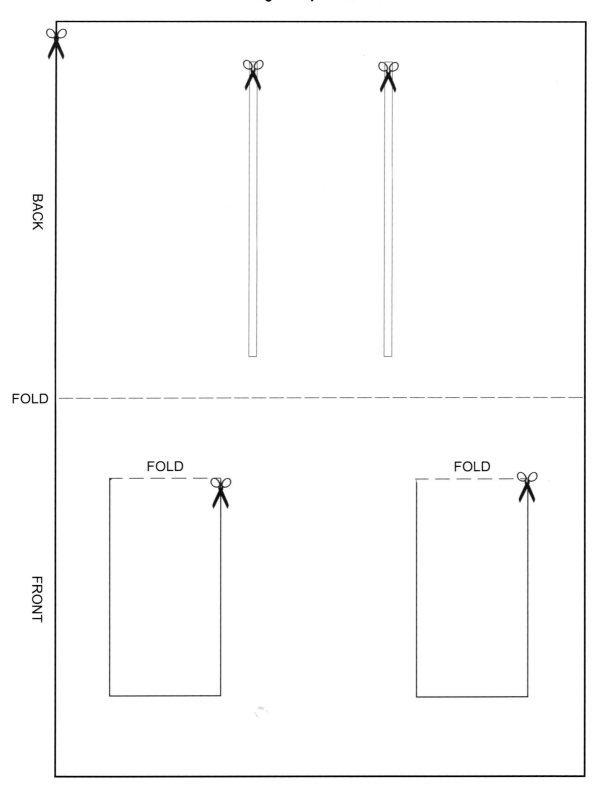

Drum Tube ★

The Drum Tube is a magical item that reveals two wonderful surprises. One end of the tube has colorful scarves or ribbons that are pulled out of thin air, and the other end magically pours out delicious candies! It's a fun way to engage with your audience and make your magic show extra special.

This trick is a little "trickier" to perform, but with some practice you'll master it in no time. Plus, think of all the candies you can eat during practice! You'll have the best excuse ever to eat tons of candies (just remember to floss and brush your teeth afterward)!

See how the Drum Tube magic trick is made and performed in this video using this QR code.
Or, visit the website: http://magictricksforkids.org/dt/

EFFECT (WHAT THE AUDIENCE SEES):

You show your audience a hollow decorative drum tube, and everyone sees that there's nothing inside. It's completely empty, and this is where the magic begins!

In front of the audience, you cover each end of the empty tube with colored tissue paper and secure rubber bands around them. Then, using your magic wand, you poke a hole through one end of the drum tube and pull out a string of colorful scarves! Wait for the stunned expressions and applause, then call up an audience member and ask them to hold out their hands in a cupped position.

To top off the magic trick, you poke the other end of the tube and, this time, candies pour out into the person's open hands. Watch as your audience smiles and relishes in the candies you've given them from your magic trick!

YOU WILL NEED:

- Decorative tape
- Magician's scarves
- Candy
- Any large prop for the table, e.g., a magician's hat
- Magic wand (page 49–50, **steps 1–2**)

- Cardboard tube
- 2 clear plastic cups
- Tissue paper (of a single color)
- Scissors
- Glue stick
- Can opener
- 4 rubber bands
- Colored paper
- Decorative stickers, beads, buttons, etc.

Tips:

- Plastic cups are the best for this trick as they are easy to cut through. Ask an adult to help if you find it difficult to make the first cut.
- To get an empty cardboard tube, use cardboard tubes that hold snacks, such as a Pringles tube.
- The cup should be able to fit in the cardboard tube, with the cup's rim stopping right at the rim of the tube so the whole cup doesn't go in.

MAKING THE TRICK:

STEP 1

Remove the bottom of the cardboard tube with a can opener. You may need some help from an adult with this bit. Make sure there are no sharp edges. With the bottom removed, you now have the perfect tube.

STEP 2

The next step is to decorate the tube.

Spread glue over the back of a colored piece of paper with a glue stick. Try to cover the whole area—if you just glue the edges, you might get bubbles in the middle when you paste it on the tube.

STEP 3

Paste the colored paper around the tube. Don't worry if your paper doesn't cover the whole tube from top to bottom. Use decorative tape or strips of different colored paper to cover the bits that are uncovered.

STEP 4

Decorate your tube however you want with decorative tape, stickers, beads, buttons, or anything else for

a magical look. I have found that electrical tape works really well as it is a bit stretchy and gives you a very smooth finish. Take your time with this bit, because this is what your audience will be looking at.

STEP 5

Fill one clear plastic cup with magician's scarves. You will have to squeeze them in to fit as much as possible.

Fill the other plastic cup with candies of your choice.

STEP 6

Cut four squares out of your colored tissue paper, about 8x8 inches big. Each tissue paper is very thin and tears easily, so be careful when doing this step.

STEP 7

Place one of the tissue paper squares on top of one of the plastic cups. Take a rubber band and fit it over the paper around the rim of the cup. Take care when you do this as tissue paper rips easily. You can ask someone to help by holding the paper down while you put the band over the tube.

Then, repeat with the other plastic cup. The cups should look a bit like a drum (that's why this trick is called the "Drum Tube").

STEP 8

Trim the extra bits of tissue paper off around the rim. This is important as it will make sure the audience doesn't see the **gimmick** (the sneaky move).

HOW THE TRICK IS PERFORMED:

STEP 1
Before the performance: prepare your magician's table. You should place a large prop, for example, a magic hat, at the front of the table. Then, hide both plastic cups, one that has been filled with magician's scarves and another that has been filled with candies and covered by colored tissue paper, behind the hat so that the audience cannot see them there. The plastic cups should be placed upside-down, with the tissue paper "lid" resting on the table.

STEP 2
To begin the magic trick in front of your audience, stick your wand through the hollow drum tube to show the audience that it's empty with nothing inside.

STEP 3

Take a piece of 8x8 colored tissue paper and place it over one end of the hollow drum tube. Carefully secure in place with a rubber band.

STEP 4
Turn the drum tube over so that other end of the tube, which has not been covered yet, is on top.

Sneaky move: Now, turn the drum tube back over and, as you place it back on the table, fit the end of the drum tube that you just covered with tissue paper in **Step 3** over the plastic cup filled with magician's scarves that is hiding behind the magician's hat. You will have to push the drum tube down with some force so that the tissue paper **breaks** and the drum tube fits over the cup.

STEP 5

Cover the uncovered end of the drum tube with tissue paper and secure with a rubber band. You now have a drum tube that is covered on both ends, with a cup of magician's scarves hiding on the bottom end.

STEP 6

Grab the bottom of the drum tube carefully so the tube doesn't slip out of the cup. Turn it over so the end with the magician's scarves is now on top.

Puncture the tissue paper with your magician's wand and pull out the strings of scarves to the *ooo's* and *ahh's* from your audience.

STEP 7

When you're finished pulling out the scarves, discreetly place the other covered end of the tube over the plastic cup that is filled with candy, like you did in **Step 4**. Once again, push down with some force so the tissue paper breaks and the drum tube fits over the cup.

STEP 8

Ask an audience member to come up to your table and put their hands out in a cupped position.

Carefully grabbing the bottom of the drum tube, flip it over so the end with the candy is now on top. Puncture the tissue and pour out the candy into your volunteer's hands! Go around the room and share the candy with the rest of your audience members to thank them for their admiration.

> ## Well done!
> Take a bow, you fantastic magician!
> And eat some candy while you're at it. You deserve it!

Electric Toothpick ★

A lot of magic tricks require you to have your own stage or table and different supplies and props to complete the performance. However, the Electric Toothpick is a special trick that you can perform anywhere at any time. You can even do it at a restaurant and amaze your neighboring diners. It's a simple trick that requires nothing but toothpicks!

Watch the Electric Toothpick magic trick demonstration using this QR code.
Or, visit the website: http://magictricksforkids.org/et/

EFFECT (WHAT THE AUDIENCE SEES):

You show your audience two toothpicks and tell them that the toothpicks are made of a special kind of wood that produces electricity when you rub it against your head.

You rub the first toothpick on your head and then place the tip near the tip of the other toothpick. The electric current will surge and the resting toothpick will jump upward, as if it is charged with electricity. It's a fantastic way to bring simple, yet satisfying, entertainment to the dinner table!

YOU WILL NEED:

- 2 toothpicks

HOW THE TRICK IS PERFORMED

STEP 1
Show your audience two toothpicks. Hold one toothpick in your hand and rest the other toothpick on an edge (for example, the edge of a table or the edge of a deck of cards). Make sure that part of the resting toothpick is extending off the edge.

STEP 2
Rub the toothpick that you're holding in your hand against your hair and tell your audience that you are generating an electric current in the toothpick.

STEP 3

Sneaky move: The "electric current" happens when you "pick" the end of the electric toothpick in your hand with your middle finger's fingernail.

Use your thumb and index finger to hold the toothpick while you place the end of the toothpick on the edge of your middle finger nail. You perform the picking motion by moving your middle finger downward. Cover this sneaky move with your index finger so your audience won't see you do the picking motion.

STEP 4

Right when you touch the resting toothpick, immediately "pick" the toothpick in your hand by flicking your middle finger downward. (Remember to cover the picking motion with the rest of your hand so the audience can't see what's happening.) The resting toothpick will jump as if charged with electricity.

Moment of magic: This trick is all about timing. Hold the electric toothpick close to the resting toothpick so that their tips almost touch.

> *Well done!*
> This is a one of the easiest magic tricks to perform.
> It can be done anywhere, as long as you have toothpicks and an edge for them to hang over.

Floating Glass ★

Do you believe in genies? Even if you don't, you'll get your audience to believe in them with the Floating Glass magic trick! This trick creates a sense of awe and mystery when you magically levitate a cup that has been filled with water. All you'll need are some simple tools to bring this magic trick to life.

Watch the video for this *genie-us* Floating Glass magic trick using this QR code.
Or, visit the website: http://magictricksforkids.org/fg/

EFFECT (WHAT THE AUDIENCE SEES):

You show the audience a decorated clear plastic cup that is half full of water and tell them that an invisible underwater genie lives inside. In your other hand, you have a piece of rope and you dip the end of the rope into the cup of water.

You ask the underwater genie to help you hold up the rope and keep it straight as you let go of the rope. However, the genie won't help you and the rope flops down. Holding up the rope again, you ask the genie to hold up the rope, but the genie doesn't do as he's told. Helpless, you hold up the rope again and turn to the audience as your other hand carelessly lets go of the cup.

You are suddenly interrupted by loud gasps and expressions of surprise when your audience sees that your cup is floating in midair! The genie has finally appeared, and you've just defied gravity with this amazing trick. Let your audience applause you and the genie for your levitation skills!

YOU WILL NEED:

- Clear plastic cup
- Scissors
- Electrical tape
- Decorative tape
- Sticky tape
- White paper clip
- Thumbtack
- Eraser
- Pliers
- Mono filament or fishing gut
- Thick piece of white cotton rope, about 12 inches long

Tips:

This cool magic trick is well worth the effort. Take your time and make it carefully for the best effect. There are some tricky bits that require an adult's help, so have a grownup nearby.

- Be careful when working with the thumbtack. Take extra care when using the pliers.
- Use a soft plastic cup for the best results.
- The rope that works best for this is called magician's rope. It is a cotton rope that has been cored. Magician's rope is available on the Internet from many different shops. Ask a grownup to help you get one.
- The mono filament that is used to make this trick is often used to make jewelry, so you can get it from most craft shops. You can also use lightweight fishing gut from an angling shop.

MAKING THE TRICK:

STEP 1

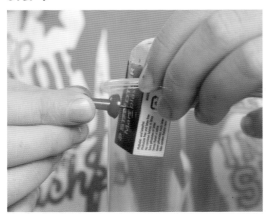

Make two small holes near the top of the plastic cup, about a half inch below the rim of the cup. We have found that the best way to make a neat hole is to use a thumbtack and an eraser.

Place the thumbtack on the outside of the cup and the eraser on the inside and press the thumbtack through the cup.

STEP 2

Repeat **step 1**, on the other side of the cup opposite the first hole. This is important because if the holes aren't exactly in the middle of the cup, the finished effect will

not be as successful. Ask for help if you are struggling with this step.

STEP 3

Thread a length of the mono filament (about 12 inches) through the holes. You need a steady hand for this! Start on the outside of the first hole and thread through the inside of the opposite hole and out on the other side. Your cup should now be able to hang in mid air if you hold the two ends of the mono filament.

STEP 4

STEP 6

Tie the two ends of the mono filament together. Make sure to tie the knot nice and tight, using a double, double knot, for example. The thread that is stretched across the top of the cup needs to be tight.

This mono filament thread is where you will "hook" the cotton rope onto. Thanks to this little string, you can make the cup float.

STEP 5

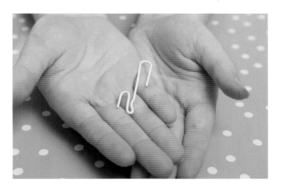

Decorate the top of the cup with some colorful tape. This decorative tape should cover the mono filament so that the audience cannot see the very thin string. The tape also adds a magical touch.

The "hook" will make the cup float. This is done with a paper clip, the **gimmick**. Twist the paper clip and bend it into the shape of a hook, as shown in the pictures. Snip off one of the ends with pliers. You may need help from an adult with this step.

STEP 7

Now, you need to measure where the paper clip should go into the rope. Place the rope inside the cup and lift it about ½–1 inch from the bottom of the cup. Mark where it meets the mono filament on the rope with your finger. This is the place where we are going to put the hook into the rope.

Tip:

Follow the steps in the pictures to stop the ends of your ropes from fraying. This will allow you to use this trick again and again. To do this, wrap see-through sticky tape around the rope ends and snip off the excess rope.

STEP 8

Push the long end of the paper clip hook into the mark in the rope in **step 7**. Make sure that the hook is *pointing downward* into the cup (inside the rope) so that the paper clip hook can hook onto the mono filament.

HOW THE TRICK IS PERFORMED:

STEP 1

Fill the paper cup with water until half full.

Introduce your audience to the invisible underwater genie and tell them that he is living in the water in your cup.

STEP 2

Holding the cup in one hand and holding the cotton rope in the other, dip the rope halfway into the cup. Tell the audience that the underwater genie will help you to hold up the rope so that it stands on its own.

Let go of the rope, and it will flop down as if the genie didn't help you.

This act is a diversion that you are using to distract the audience from the main trick of the floating cup, so that it will have a larger and more surprising effect.

Tip
Whenever you hold the rope, hold it such that the audience cannot see the hook that is sticking out of the rope.

STEP 3

Repeat **step 2**, holding the rope up and letting the rope flop down again. Pretend to be disappointed in the genie and explain to the audience that the genie couldn't hear your call for help since he is underwater.

Sneaky move: As you explain this bit to the audience, hold the rope straight up in the cup again. However, this time discreetly hook the end of the paper clip that is attached to your rope onto the thin mono filament. At the same time, let go of the cup.

STEP 4

Moment of magic: The cup is now "floating" in midair, held up only by the rope!

You can awe your audience even more by pouring more water to the cup, or gently swinging the cup round and round.

Well Done

You have mastered the Floating Cup magic trick.

Your audience will wonder, "How can this amazing genie magician fool gravity like that?!"

Growing Magic Wand ★

You're a famous magician who does grand magic tricks, but your wand has shrunk! What can you do to turn it back into a big wand? Well, with the Growing Magic Wand trick, you'll get your big wand back in no time, and you'll floor your audience with your magic skills. This trick is a great way to start off your magic show, especially since you'll need a large wand, not a tiny one, to do all your magic performances.

Watch the Growing Magic Wand trick in action using this QR code.
Or, visit the website: http://magictricksforkids.org/gw/

EFFECT (WHAT THE AUDIENCE SEES):

You share a story about how your magic wand has shrunk to the size of a toothpick and show your audience an itty-bitty wand inside your little magic bag. But, because you're the best magician in the world, you can reverse your small magic wand and turn it into a big wand for your big magic tricks!

You wave your fingers above your magic bag, open it, and pull out the big magic wand! Your audience will applaud your incredible, jaw-dropping skills.

YOU WILL NEED:

Tips:
- Buy a new coin purse for your magic show, use a coin purse you already have, or ask permission to use an old one from any ladies in your family. You will have to cut a hole in your coin purse, so make sure everyone is okay with that! A decorative coin purse is better since it'll add a magical touch.
- Remember to cover your work area with old news-paper and wear old clothes when you do painting.

- Dowel stick or rod (about 0.5 inch in diameter, 15 inches in length)
- Dowel stick or rod (about 0.2 inch in diameter, 4 inches in length)
- Hacksaw
- Masking tape
- Black poster paint
- White poster paint
- Paintbrush or craft brush (0.5 inch in diameter)
- Scissors
- White paper
- See-through sticky tape
- Small coin purse
- Old newspaper and old clothes

MAKING THE TRICK:

STEP 1

To make your big magic wand, cut the thicker dowel stick (0.5 inch in diameter) to a length of about 15 inches using a hacksaw. Ask a grownup for help if you find it tricky.

STEP 2

Wrap a piece of masking tape around each end of the dowel stick. Paint the dowel stick with black poster paint. Leave to dry. Paint another coat if you need to.

Once the black paint is dry, remove the masking tape and paint the tips with white poster paint. Leave to dry. Paint another coat if you need to.

STEP 3

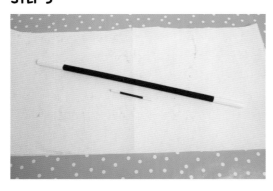

To make your mini magic wand, cut the thinner dowel stick (0.2 inch in diameter) to a length of about 4 inches using a hacksaw. Ask a grownup for help if you find it tricky.

STEP 4

Repeat **steps 1–2** with the thin dowel stick, and you have a mini magic wand.

STEP 5

Cut a small hole in the bottom corner of a coin purse. The big magic wand needs to be able to fit comfortably through the hole.

HOW THE TRICK IS PERFORMED:

STEP 1

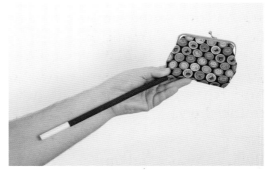

Before the performance: Insert the tip of the big magic wand through the hole in the coin purse and hide the rest of the wand behind your hand and entire arm as shown. It is important to watch your angles when you do this so that your audience doesn't see the wand behind your arm. Keep this position throughout the performance, with your arm around the magic wand that is inserted into the coin purse.

You must also place the mini magic wand inside the coin purse. You are ready to begin.

STEP 2

Tell the audience a story of how your magic wand shrunk. Be creative! For example, your mother washed your wand with the laundry, which caused it to shrink, or another magician or a fairy pulled a prank on you and shrunk your wand. When you tell your story, be expressive and have fun! It'll add more entertainment to the show.

STEP 3

Pull the mini wand out of the purse and show it to the audience. Then, drop it back into your magic bag. Close the purse, wave your hand and fingers above it, say some magic words, and open the purse again.

To **produce** the big magic wand, simply pull it out from the hole in

Terms:

Angles, in magic, refers to the angle or direction from which your audience is watching your performance. Some tricks like this one require special attention to the direction from which your audience is watching the trick, to make sure the secret stays hidden.

To **produce** or to do a **production** is to make something appear as if by magic.

Flashing is when a magician unintentionally shows something that is secretly hidden—in this case, the wand that is hidden behind your arm.

the corner of your purse, all the time making sure your audience doesn't see the wand hiding behind your arm. If they do see it, the magic trick is revealed by accident and this is called **flashing**.

Look at your audience and watch their faces light up in awe!

Haunted Vase Illusion ★

Don't be fooled by the title! This magic trick is anything but spooky and scary. It's fun and entertaining for both magician and audience. With the Haunted Vase Illusion, you'll be able to summon a real-life (but friendly!) ghost to help you with a superb magic trick.

Enjoy the video tutorial for the Haunted Vase Illusion magic trick using this QR code.
Or, visit the website: http://magictricksforkids.org/hv/

EFFECT (WHAT THE AUDIENCE SEES):

You have an invisible friendly ghost who lives in a vase. You show your audience that nothing is inside the vase.

You hold the vase and place part of the cotton rope inside it. When you flip the vase over, the rope doesn't fall out because your ghostly friend is holding onto it for you! What a loyal pal you have there.

Then, to show the audience that the ghost is still there, flip the vase over and hold onto the rope that is hanging out of the vase. The vase will start to swing from side to side without falling to the ground! Your audience will love this levitating trick and applaud you and your ghostly buddy.

YOU WILL NEED:

- Small opaque vase with a very narrow neck
- Piece of thick cotton rope (about 8 inches long)
- See-through sticky tape
- Scissors
- Eraser

MAKING THE TRICK:

STEP 1

Prepare your piece of rope (about 8 inches long). To prevent from fraying, wrap see-through sticky tape around the rope ends and snip off the excess rope (see step-by-step pictures in the "Tips" box on page 44).

Tips:

It takes about 10 minutes to make your props for the Haunted Vase Illusion and the effect is awesome.

- The rope we use is called magician's rope. It is cotton rope that has been cored. Magician's rope is available on the Internet from many different shops.
- The success of this trick lies in the kind of vase you use. Firstly, it needs to be colored glass; a clear glass vase won't work. Secondly, the neck, or the opening of the vase, needs to be very narrow. Look at the vase that we have used and find something similar. You can find vases in thrift stores.

STEP 2

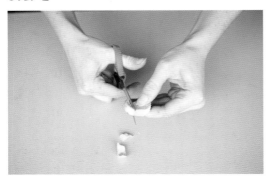

The next step is to make the **gimmick**—this is the secret bit that the audience doesn't know about. Cut the eraser into the shape of a little ball. It needs to be just a little bit smaller than the thinnest part of the vase's opening or neck, but large enough to catch the rope when it is placed beside it in the vase's neck. Both the eraser and the rope shouldn't move when placed together.

Measure your eraser as you trim small bits away at a time. Be careful not to cut it too small.

Well done!
That's it! You are now ready to perform the Haunted Vase Illusion!

HOW THE TRICK IS PERFORMED:

STEP 1
Tell the audience that have a friendly ghost who lives in the vase. The ghost has agreed to help you with your magic performance, but since he is shy, he won't materialize or reveal himself to anyone. Show your audience that nothing is inside the vase.

STEP 2

Slip the little ball into the vase without your audience noticing. To distract them, you can pass the rope around the room so the audience can make sure it is a "real" rope and not a "trick" rope. While they are concentrated on the rope, slip the ball in.

STEP 3

Moment of magic: Now, place the rope into the vase. Tip the vase upside down so that the ball rolls into the neck of the vase and traps the rope so it stays in place.

Now, the rope will not fall out from the vase because of your ghostly friend's help.

STEP 4

To show that the ghost is still there, flip the vase back over. Hold the rope with one hand and release the vase. The vase will now float in midair, and you can even swing it gently from side to side! Thank your ghostly friend for helping you in this gravity-defing trick.

To make your performance more believable and engage the audience, you can also ask an audience member to hold onto the rope for you.

Tips:

After your performance, if you want to release the rope from the vase, gently push the rope into the vase to let the eraser ball fall to the base. Now, the rope is free to come out. You can also discreetly remove your gimmick (without your audience noticing) and hand the vase and the rope out to your crowd for inspection.

Healing Rope ★

You love skipping rope, but your rope has now been divided into three pieces! What can you do? Oh, but you're the fantastic magician who can make the impossible possible. With a single rope and two shorter rope pieces, you can easily trick your audience and put your divided rope back together again. It'll take a bit of practice to get the steps right, but you're a magician—you can do it!

Watch the video demonstration of the Healing Rope trick using this QR code.
Or, visit the website: http://magictricksforkids.org/rt/

EFFECT (WHAT THE AUDIENCE SEES):

You have a rope that looks like it's been cut into three equal pieces. One end is knotted so that the three pieces are tied together, while the three pieces on the other end hang loose.

In front of the audience you tie a knot with two of the loose strands. Then, on the knotted end, you untie the knot and let the three strands loose. On that newly loosened end, you tie a knot between two strands. Then, you extend the rope and it now looks like one full rope joined together with two knots.

But no one wants a knotted rope, right? So, to magically release the knots, you ask someone from the audience to blow on the knots one at time. Pull on the rope, and the knots will come loose. You've fixed your cut-up rope and made it whole again!

YOU WILL NEED:

- Piece of soft cotton rope (magician's rope), about 60 inches long
- Scissors
- See-through sticky tape

Tips:
The best rope for this rope trick is called magician's rope. It is cotton rope and the core has been removed. Magician's rope is easy to find on the Internet and you can ask a grown-up to help you find it online.

MAKING THE TRICK:

STEP 1
Cut a length of rope measuring about 40 inches. It needs to be long enough so that you can hold on to each end when you stretch your arms from side to side.

STEP 2
Cut two smaller pieces, about 8 inches long each.

STEP 3

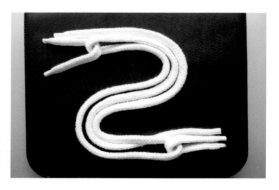

The long rope gets folded into three almost equal lengths. The ends of the long rope stick out a little bit

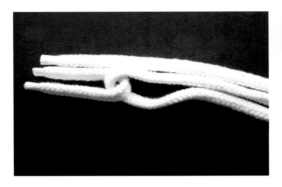

past the folded loops. Insert the two smaller pieces of rope through the folded loops in the longer rope, as shown in the picture. This will create the appearance of three loose strands, completing the illusion that you have three separate pieces of rope of the same length.

STEP 4

Tie the ropes into a big knot at both ends so that the little loops are hidden. This is your starting position.

HOW THE TRICK IS PERFORMED:

STEP 1

Tell the audience a story about how your favorite rope got cut up into three equal pieces. You can be creative here and say, for example, that a dinosaur wanted to floss with your rope, but broke it into pieces instead. You were so mad that you sent the dinosaur back to history again. See? Your story can make your show totally fun. Prepare a story ahead of time and rehearse how you'll tell it.

Show the audience the rope, which has been knotted at both ends. Then, inform your audience that as a magician you have the skills to transform all three pieces back into one single rope.

STEP 2

Untie a knot on one of the ends. Be careful as you untie them because you don't want to drop the little ropes and reveal your secret to the audience. Hide the small rope that is looped around the large rope behind your hand.

STEP 3

Sneaky move: Now, tie the ends of the small rope together in a knot, although from the audience's perspective it appears that you are tying a knot between the two long strands of rope.

When you tie the knot, do not knot the small rope around the long rope such that the long rope is going through the small rope's knot. Instead, pinch the loop of the long rope together and knot the small rope around the top of the loop of the long rope.

Tip:

This trick takes a bit of practice to get the handling right. Make sure the loop is small so you don't **flash** them and reveal your secret. **Flashing** is when a magician shows something that is secretly hidden by accident; in this case, the loop and the small pieces of rope.

STEP 4

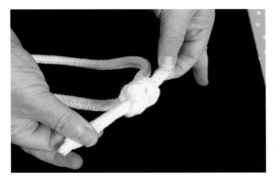

Turn the rope upside down and repeat **steps 2–3** on the other end.

STEP 5

You should now have a rope that looks like three shorter pieces of rope have been knotted together.

Moment of magic: Grab onto the rope on either side of one of the knots. Then, blow onto the knot and pull the rope tight at the same time. (The blow is for added magical effect and doesn't really do anything, but it looks cool!)

When you pull the rope tight, the knot will jump straight off the rope! How amazing!

STEP 6

Now repeat **step 5** with the other knot. You can even have an audience member do the "magic blow" so your trick is more believable.

Well done!
You have restored three separate pieces of rope into one long piece of rope.

Key-Bending Mentalism ★

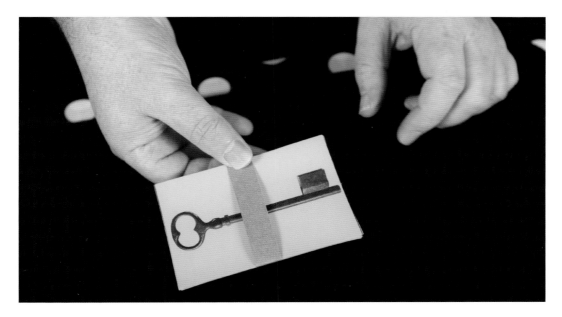

Magicians love to use their mental powers for all sorts of magic tricks because the mind is a powerful tool. As a superstar magician, you can put your magical mind to work with the Key-Bending Mentalism magic trick!

Watch the video for the Key-Bending Mentalism trick using this QR code.
Or, visit the website: http://magictricksforkids.org/kb/

EFFECT (WHAT THE AUDIENCE SEES):

You have a pack of cards with keys printed on them. The pack is tied together with a band. You call for a volunteer and ask them to sign their name on the front and back of the first key card. You place the key in the person's hand, face down, and ask your assistant to put their other hand on top of the key.

After you wave your magic wand over it, you flip the card over and reveal that the key has been bent with your mental powers! It's also the key that has your assistant's signature on it. Your audience will be completely bewildered by this incredible magic trick.

YOU WILL NEED:

- A4- or letter-sized sheet of colored card paper
- Scissors
- Strip of paper (of a different color)
- See-through sticky tape/glue stick
- Printout of the keys (page 64)

MAKING THE TRICK:

STEP 1

Using the printout provided on page 64, print the keys out on a piece of colored card paper.

> ### Tips:
> You can also print the keys on regular paper, but you will need to stick a second piece of blank paper on the back as you don't want the printed keys to show through the paper when you turn it around.

STEP 2

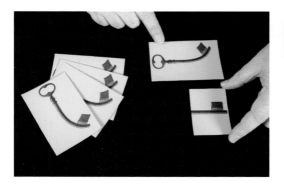

Cut out all the keys along the printed lines.

Cut the straight key along the dotted line. You will only use the bottom part of that key, as shown in the picture.

STEP 3

Neatly stack all the cut out keys into a pack, making sure all the keys face the same way.

STEP 4

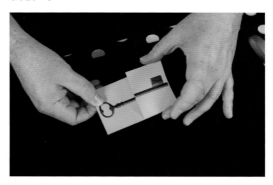

Place the "half" card with the straight key stem on the top of the pile of keys.

STEP 5

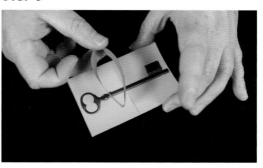

Make a paper band that fits neatly around your pack of keys. Use a different color for the paper band as it adds an extra element of misdirection.

Tips:

If you are using very thick card paper, a thick elastic band will also work.

STEP 6

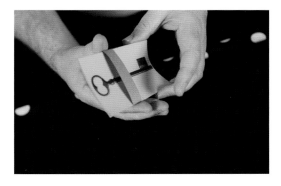

Now slide the paper band around the pack of keys. Use it to hide the edge of the cut straight key.

You now have a pack of key cards. Each card has a bent key printed on it, but you've made the first key look straight, and it appears that the whole pack consists of all straight keys.

Well done!

You are ready to perform the Key-Bending Mentalism trick where you will bend a key in an audience member's hand.

HOW THE TRICK IS PERFORMED:

STEP 1

Ask your assistant to sign their name on the first key card to prove that it really is their key. They have to sign on the top half of the card and not the bottom half, because that is the removable part!

STEP 2

Sneaky move: Flip over the pack of keys. When you flip it over, with your fingers holding onto the top half of the first key card that your assistant just signed, pull it out from the pack.

Place the key card face down on the table and ask your assistant to sign it on the back as well.

This motion of flipping the pack of cards over prevents the audience from seeing your half card.

STEP 3

Ask your assistant to hold out their hand. Place the signed card in their hand with the key image face down. Ask your assistant to place their other hand on top of the card. Make a magical movement with your wand or hands, telling your audience that you are using your magical mental powers.

Flip the card over. The card now reveals a bent key image!

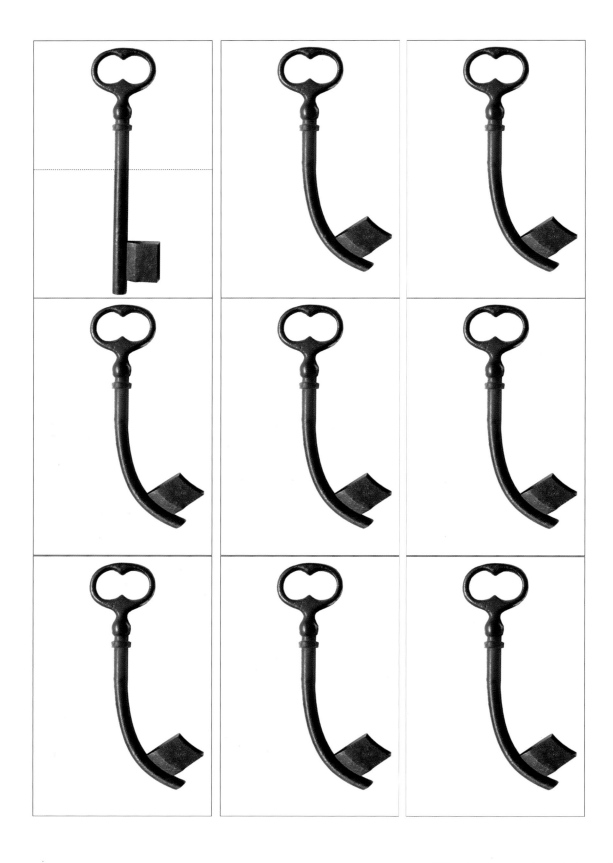

Knife-Eating Illusion ★

This is another fun, illusion-tastic magic trick that you can do in restaurants or right at home at the dinner table! It's an easy way to fool people that you've just eaten a knife, which is supposed to be impossible, right? But you're a fantastic magician and you can do the impossible.

Check out the Knife-Eating Illusion for yourself using this QR code.
Or, visit the website: http://magictricksforkids.org/ke/

EFFECT (WHAT THE AUDIENCE SEES):

The audience watches intently as you're about to eat a knife. With a big motion, you sprinkle a little salt on the knife to bring out the delicious metal flavor.

Suddenly, you shove the knife in your mouth and chew vigorously. You make a swallowing effect and open your mouth to show your audience that it's empty. Your audience will go mad and wonder how you just ate a knife!

YOU WILL NEED:

- Knife
- Salt shaker

Tips:
The Knife-Eating Illusion is a great trick to perform at a restaurant or a dinner party. This trick is all about your timing and the body language you use to attract attention to yourself and away from the knife.

HOW THE TRICK IS PERFORMED:

STEP 1
First, hold the knife up to your face with your hands almost covering the entire knife. Leave a space open so people can see the knife. Look around you and act like you don't want people to see you eat the knife (this would help especially if you're in a restaurant).

The trick is to direct your audience's attention elsewhere. You don't want your audience to focus solely on the knife, because you'll drop the knife in your lap in the next step.

STEP 2
Bring your knife up toward your mouth as if you're about to eat it. But, wait! You want to add some salt to the knife, so use your salt shaker and sprinkle lots of salt on the knife. Make a big motion here and let the salt rain down on your knife and table. This big motion is a great attention grabber and focuses the audience's attention on you and away from the knife.

STEP 3
Secretly hide your knife even more in your hands by covering most of the knife with your fingers and palms. A very small part of the knife should be revealed.

Bring your knife toward your mouth again, but then look left and right, checking to see that no one is watching you. As you do this, move your hands and knife near your lap until they are just level with the edge of the table, making sure your audience can still see part of your hands.

STEP 4
Sneaky move: Quickly drop the knife in your lap, then shove your hands into your mouth, pretending that you have stuffed the knife inside. Act like you're chewing on the knife and talk to your audience with your mouth full.

You can even make a joke here, such as "Knives are healthy for you, you know! They're full of iron!" It's a great way to end the magic show and wrap up the illusion.

Tips:
Have a paper napkin on your lap—this helps to catch the knife when you drop it and stops it from slipping off your lap.

Well done!
You have learned how to do the Knife-Eating Illusion.

Make a name for yourself with this comical routine.

Linking Paper Clips ★

Paper clips can do more than just hold piles of paper together! The paper clips you'll use in this magic trick won't just be any ordinary paper clips, either. Since you're a wonderful magician, you'll make them do the magic for you during your performance.

Watch the Linking Paper Clips magic trick unfold in this video using this QR code.
Or, visit the website: http://magictricksforkids.org/lpc/

EFFECT (WHAT THE AUDIENCE SEES):

You have a folded piece of paper with one paper clip on each fold. You pull the paper to unfold it at a fast speed and the paper clips jump in the air. You pick up the paper clips and show the audience that they've been linked during the jump. Beam at the audience and take your bow!

YOU WILL NEED:

- 2 standard paper clips
- Paper money or a piece of paper

Tips:

The Linking Paper Clips magic trick is a brilliant impromptu trick and can be performed anywhere as long as you have paper and paper clips. Impromptu magic is good fun as you do magic with everyday objects that can be handed out for examination before and after you do the trick. The effect of the linking paper clips is called a penetration.

HOW THE TRICK IS PERFORMED:

STEP 1

Take your paper note or piece of paper and fold it into an "s" shape as shown in the pictures.

STEP 2

Place the first paper clip onto the note as shown in the pictures. You want to join the front of the note (from the audience's point of view) with the first fold of the "s" shape.

STEP 3

Place the second paper clip on the note as shown in the pictures, joining the second fold of the "s" shape with the back of the note (from the audience's point of view).

STEP 4

Moment of magic: Holding the ends of the note or piece of paper between your forefingers and thumbs, pull the ends in opposite directions so as to unfold the note. This causes the paper clips to slide towards one another and then, as the note fully opens up, the paper clips will link together as if by magic!

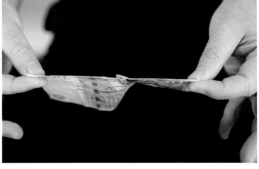

Well done!

You have performed the Linking Paper Clip trick.

Enjoy performing this trick for friends and family wherever you are.

Magic Bowling Pin Illusion ★

Score a strike with your audience with the Magic Bowling Pin Illusion! This trick is a great spin-off of a regular game of bowling, and you don't even need to keep score. You can even do this during a bowling party to entertain your friends and family!

Watch the video for the Magic Bowling Pin Illusion using this QR code.
Or, visit the website: http://magictricksforkids.org/mbp/

EFFECT (WHAT THE AUDIENCE SEES):

You have two decorated hollow tubes. Two bowling pins are placed inside these empty tubes.

Your assistant will pick any one of the bowling pins and tubes, and you will have the other bowling pin and tube. Together, you and your assistant will hold onto your individual tubes with both hands clasped over the ends to keep the bowling pin in. At the same time, you both turn your tube over three times, then lift the tube slightly to reveal the bowling pin underneath.

Surprise! Your bowling pin is facing one way, but your assistant's bowling pin faces the other way. This will confuse the audience, since you both turned the tube over three times together.

Now, you repeat the process with your partner. But the results are still the same—your bowling pins are facing opposite directions! How can this happen? Even when you try the process a third time, the results are still the same. Your crowd will be confused by and impressed with this illusion.

YOU WILL NEED:

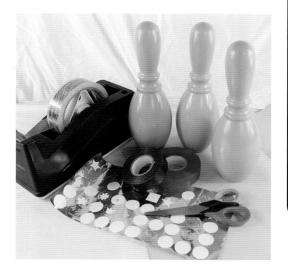

Tips:

The Magic Bowling Pin Illusion is performed with an audience member. This is really good fun, because they keep getting it wrong . . .

Making the trick is easy enough, but you may need to ask a grown-up for help with cutting the **gimmicked** bowling pin.

- 2 sheets of A3-sized card, about 11.5 x 16.5 inches (different colors)
- 3 plastic hollow bowling pins (the same color)
- Scissors
- See-through sticky tape
- Decorative stickers and tape

MAKING THE TRICK:

STEP 1

Place a bowling pin on an A3-sized card and roll the card around it to form a tube.

Tips:
Make sure that you roll the card loosely around the bowling pin to allow it to easily drop out of the tube when you turn it upright.

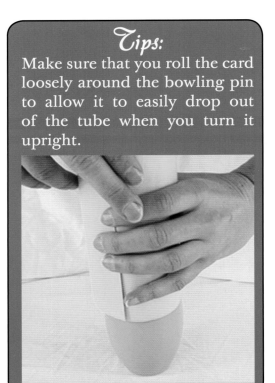

STEP 2

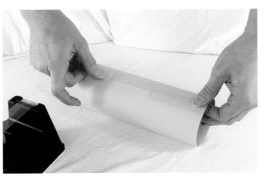

Using the see-through sticky tape, stick the card down to make the tube and keep it in place.

STEP 3
Repeat **steps 1–2** with the second piece of card to make another tube.

STEP 4

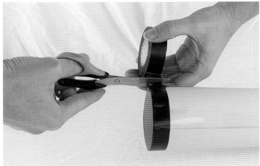

Stick decorative tape around the top and bottom edges of both the tubes. Use only one color for the top and bottom of a tube. You can use a different color for the other tube, as long as the top and bottom of each tube matches.

STEP 5

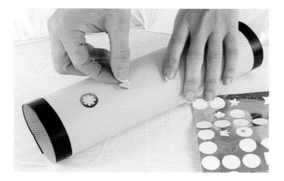

Now it is time for the artsy bit. Decorate your tubes. We chose stickers, but you can paint or draw on the tubes in any way you like.

STEP 6

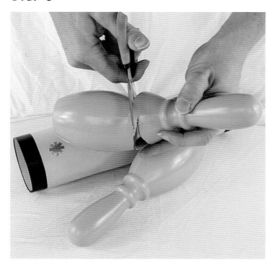

Making the **gimmick** is a bit tricky and you may need some help here. We are going to cut the "neck" off one of the three bowling pins. Getting started is quite difficult, so ask an adult to make a hole so that you can get your scissors into the bowling pin to do the cutting.

You won't need the neck bit so you can throw that away. The bottom bit is the **gimmick** for this trick. The bottom should be able to fit over the top of another bowling pin and sit there.

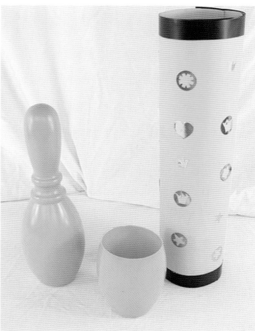

HOW THE TRICK IS PERFORMED:

STEP 1

You'll be using two tubes and two and a half bowling pins. To prepare for the trick, place one tube over one bowling pin on the table.

Now, place the bottom half of the bowling pin (your **gimmick**) over the top of the other bowling pin, and place the second tube over it. This is your tube. As you handle this tube throughout the performance, you have to practice holding it in such a way that you are also holding onto the gimmick at the same time. Squeeze the tube gently to grab the gimmick, so whenever you lift up the tube, you will also be lifting up the gimmick. Don't be too obvious or your audience will notice that you're holding onto something!

> *Tip:*
> The gimmick is the part that the audience doesn't see, so make sure you don't give it to your assistant!

STEP 2

An audience member or your assistant will help you with this magic trick. Ask them to choose any bowling pin they want. (However, don't let them choose the tube!)

Then, standing side by side, both of you will place your tubes over the individual bowling pins and get ready to begin (remember that as you hold your tube, you are also holding onto the gimmick). Once your tube is over the bowling pin, you can let go.

STEP 3

Both you and your assistant will place your hands on either end of the tube. Tell your assistant to flip the tube upside down three times, together with you. Count "1, 2, 3" for each turn.

Then, lift your tube slightly to reveal the bowling pin underneath. Do not lift the tube all the way! Your tube should reveal the rounded bottom of the bowling pin, while your assistant's tube will reveal the top tip of the bowling pin.

STEP 4

Pretend that your assistant made a mistake and tell them to do it again with you. Make a joke to your audience, saying that your assistant must not be counting right.

Together, flip the tube three times with your assistant, then slowly reveal the bowling pin. This time, the gimmick is on top of the bowling pin, so you can remove the tube entirely (while pinching gently to grab onto the gimmick as well) to reveal the whole pin.

STEP 5

Repeat the flips one more time and show your audience the illusion again. Your assistant will get it "wrong" every time. Your audience will wonder how this has happened!

Milk in a Hat ★

The Milk in a Hat magic trick is very funny. In it, the audience will think that you are learning your very first magic trick from an instruction card, so this is a great one to start off your magic show!

Watch a video demonstration of the Milk in a Hat magic trick using this QR code.
Or, visit the website: http://magictricksforkids.org/mih/

EFFECT (WHAT THE AUDIENCE SEES):

You tell the audience that you are about to learn a new trick for the very first time.

The instructions for the trick are printed on a piece of paper. You read them out in a loud voice as you put a plastic cup into a hat. You then notice that the glass is not clean so you remove it from the hat, clean it, but forget to put it back in the hat.

You read the instructions again and tell the audience that you must pour milk into the cup in the hat. The audience can see that the glass is on the table and not in the hat, but you pretend not to notice. This is very funny for the audience because they think you have made a mistake.

You then notice that the glass is not in the hat. Whoops! You look into the hat, pretending that you have made a milky mess inside—this is a great opportunity for you to act as if the whole trick has gone wrong. However, you are a magician, of course! You put the glass back into the hat and wave your magic wand. Abracadabra! In the blink of an eye, the milk appears inside the glass and the hat is dry. Take your bow as the audience goes crazy with applause.

YOU WILL NEED:

- Hat
- Two plastic cups
- Scissors
- Electrical tape
- Decorative tape
- A4- or letter-sized colored cardboard
- Glue stick
- "Instructions for first trick" printout (page 83)

Tips:

- Soft plastic drinking cups are the best as they can be cut easily to make the **gimmick**. Ask an adult to help if you find it difficult to make the first cut.
- You have to find cups that are short enough to be covered fully when placed in the hat
- Electrical tape (called insulation tape) works very nicely because it is a bit stretchy and makes a smooth edge around the top of the cup. Tape that is not stretchy might crease.
- You can use any decorative tape or stickers to add a magical effect.
- The "Instructions for first trick" printout adds a comedic effect to your performance.

MAKING THE TRICK:

STEP 1

Cut the top rim off one of the plastic cups, about ½ inch from the top. Make sure to cut as neatly as you can as this will be the edge that you don't want the audience to see. Take your time and finish it off as nicely as you can.

STEP 2

Now, cut off the bottom of the other cup. I have found that this trick works best when you cut out the inside of the base (instead of cutting off the bottom). Make the cut as tidy as you can and trim the edges for a smooth finish. This cup is going to sit inside the first cup to complete the gimmick.

STEP 3

Decorate your plastic cup gimmick. Cut a length of electrical tape.

Carefully stick the tape around the top of the cup with the bottom cut out. Use the rim as a guide and you'll have a really straight line. You want a tidy finish as this bit of decoration is going to help hide the sneaky move from your audience.

STEP 4

Place the cup with the bottom cut out inside the cup with the top cut off. This is the trick cup that is made up of two parts with one fitting inside the other. The two cups nest together and give the illusion of one perfect plastic cup.

Trim the edge of the cup on the outside (the one with the top cut off) to line up with the bottom edge of the tape, as shown in the picture. This will hide the sneaky move.

STEP 5

Decorate the electrical tape around the edge of the cup with stickers or colorful tape. This adds a magical effect and will also help to distract your audience. This is called **misdirection**.

STEP 6

Take the "Instructions for first trick" printout and cut neatly around the outside of the blue line. You can leave a little white border if you want to.

STEP 7

Glue the back of the cutout with a glue stick. Make sure to cover the whole area, not just the borders.

This will help you get a smooth and flat finish. Stick the cutout on a colored A4- or letter-sized cardboard.

Tips:

If you put the finished "Instructions for first trick" card under a heavy book or stack of magazines and leave it to dry for a couple of hours, you get a really flat finish.

HOW THE TRICK IS PERFORMED:

STEP 1
Tell the audience that you are about to learn a new trick for the very first time and instructions are printed on the "Instructions for first trick" card. You read the instructions aloud as you perform the trick.

STEP 2
Place the two nested plastic cups into the hat (the audience thinks it's just one ordinary cup but you know it's made of two parts).

Then, pretend that you forgot to clean the cup. When you remove the cup from the hat for a clean, secretly leave the outside cup (the one without a top rim) in the hat and only remove the inside cup (the one without a bottom). Whenever you handle the bottomless cup, hold it carefully so that the audience can't see that it doesn't have a bottom.

Clean the bottomless cup and put it back on the table (you are pretending to forget to put it back into the hat).

STEP 3
Continue to read the instructions. While you focus your attention on the card, pour the milk into the hidden cup in the hat. However, the audience only sees the cup on the table, so they think you are accidentally pouring milk directly into the hat!

This is where you get to have fun! Act as if you have made a mistake. Remember, a magician is really an actor playing the part of a magician.

STEP 4

Now, it's time to prove you are a real magician.

Pick up the bottomless cup (once again, be careful not to show the audience that it doesn't have a bottom) and place it back inside the cup in the hat. It should fit neatly inside the cup with the milk without spilling any.

STEP 5

Grab a magic wand (you can learn how to make one on page 49–50, **steps 1–2**) and say some magic words.

Remove your trick cup (be careful to hold up both cups) and the audience will see it is full of milk. Show the audience that the hat is dry by putting it on your head.

Take a big bow and thank your audience for the big round of applause.

Well done!
Have fun amazing everyone with this easy magic trick!

Instructions for first trick

Monkey Bar ★

Your audience will go bananas over the Monkey Bar magic trick! With just three colorful ribbons and a monkey bar, you can create an optical illusion and make jaws drop.

Watch the secrets behind the Monkey Bar magic trick in this video using this QR code.
Or, visit the website: http://magictricksforkids.org/mb/

EFFECT (WHAT THE AUDIENCE SEES):

Three ribbons hang from a monkey bar: a blue ribbon on the right-hand side and two orange ribbons in the middle and on the left-hand side.

You tell your audience that you can transfer the blue ribbon from the right side to the left. But everyone's thinking (or saying), "Oh, but the magician can just turn the monkey bar quickly to the other side!" You act insulted and decide to show them who's boss! You yank hard on the ribbons and voilà! The blue ribbon magically leaps to the middle! Your amazing magical talent will shock your audience.

YOU WILL NEED:

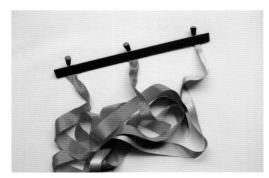

- Ribbon, two colors (40 inches of one color and 80 inches of another color)
- Slide binder
- 3 plastic cord end caps with tops

> ### *Tips:*
> You can get the slide binder from a stationery store. The cord end caps and ribbons can be found at fabric shops.
>
> You may need some help from a grownup with a few of the steps.

MAKING THE TRICK:

STEP 1

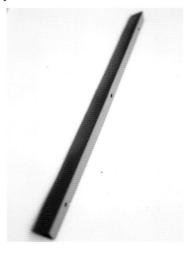

Ask a grownup to help you make three holes in the slide binder. I used a handheld drill and a small drill bit (2–3 mm). Make the holes at equal distances from each other on the top of the slide binder.

> ### *Tips:*
> Measure and find the middle of the slide binder. Mark this as your middle hole. Measure equal distances to the left and right of the middle hole (leave about ½ inch from the ends) and mark the other two holes. Now make the holes on the marks. Make sure the holes are smooth as the ribbon will be traveling through these holes and might catch on any rough patches.

STEP 2

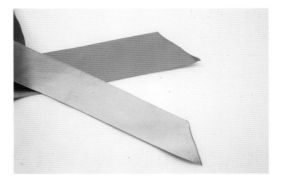

Cut your ribbons—two 40-inch pieces of one color (orange) and one 40-inch piece of another color (blue). Cut the ends at a 45 degree angle. This stops the ribbon from fraying.

STEP 3

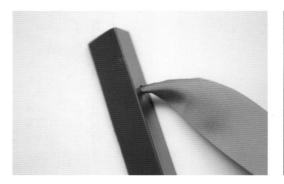

Now feed the first of the two similarly colored ribbons (orange) through one of the holes on the end of the slide binder.

> ### *Tip:*
> Use a pencil to open the slide binder to make it easier to get the ribbon through.

STEP 4

Feed a cord end cap onto the end of the ribbon that sticks out above the slide binder. Make a knot right near the end of the ribbon above the cord end cap. Pull the ribbon into the cord end cap. The knot stops it from pulling through the cap.

STEP 5

Put the lid on the cord end cap. This gives a neat finish to your monkey bar. Pull the ribbon through the slide binder so that the cord end cap sits right on top of the slide binder, as shown in the pictures.

STEP 6

Repeat **steps 3–5** with the other two ribbons.

REMEMBER: the single color ribbon (blue) goes in the middle of the slide binder.

> ***Well done!***
> You have made the Monkey Bar magic trick.

HOW THE TRICK IS PERFORMED:

STEP 1

To prepare your trick before the performance, hold the slide binder up to your face and let the ribbons hang from it. Pull upward on the blue ribbon end cap to create excess ribbon. Then, holding on to the other end of the blue ribbon, feed it through the binder and slide it to the end on the left-hand side so that the blue ribbon is now hanging out from the left end of the binder.

Similarly, pull upward on the end cap of the orange ribbon on the left of the binder to create excess ribbon. Then, holding on to the other end of the orange ribbon, feed it through the binder and slide it through toward the middle of the binder and let it hang from there. Now, the orange and blue ribbons will look like they've switched places with the blue at the end and the orange in the middle.

STEP 2

Tell your audience that you can transfer the blue ribbon from the right side to the left. With a swift motion of your hands, flip the monkey bar from one side to the other so the blue ribbon is now on the other side! This is your "decoy" trick.

Your audience should figure out that you simply turned the monkey bar from one side to the other,

and they will question your magic skills. Pretend to be insulted and ask them if they want you to magically transfer the blue ribbon to the middle instead. They'll say a big "yes!" together.

STEP 3

Moment of magic: Yank hard on the ribbons. The blue ribbon, which was hanging from the end, will magically leap to the middle while the orange ribbon will now be on the end. You made the blue and orange ribbon switch places!

For extra comedic effect, you can act like switching places is impossible to do. As you yank the ribbons, say, "See? There's no way anyone can do that!" Then, you look down at your monkey bar and act surprised that the blue ribbon has jumped to the middle!

Mystery Tube ★

Wiggle your fingers and wave your wand for the Mystery Tube magic trick! With just a small number of items, you can create a big magic show and entertain your audience with an easy but enchanting trick.

Watch how the Mystery Tube trick is performed in this video using this QR code.
Or, visit the website: http://magictricksforkids.org/mt/

EFFECT (WHAT THE AUDIENCE SEES):

You show your audience two cans, and they see that there's nothing inside. Now that you've fooled them into believing that the cans are empty, you pull out a super long ribbon hidden inside the can, shocking your audience into awe and applause.

YOU WILL NEED:

- 3 tin cans, all different sizes (see measurements in the **Measurements** section)
- Can opener
- Chalkboard paint (black)
- Paint brush or decorating brush (1 or 1.5 inches)
- Newspaper and old clothes
- Colored paper
- Scissors
- Electrical tape
- Decorative tape and stickers
- See-through sticky tape
- Black paper clip
- Pair of wire cutting pliers
- Small piece of gaffer tape
- Colored ribbons, magician's scarves, or anything else you want to put into the mystery tube

Measurements

The three cans need to fit one inside the other. Recommended measurements:

- The **largest can** is a standard soup or bean can, measuring 3 inches in diameter and 4.5 inches in height.
- The **second can** is slightly smaller. These are normally one portion soup cans, measuring 2.5 inches in diameter and 4 inches in height.
- The **third can** is used for tinned fish and measures 2 inches in diameter and 3 inches in height.

Make sure you wash all the cans thoroughly after they have been emptied. You don't want your props to smell like fish!

Tips

- Part of making this trick will involve painting (yeah!). Work in an area that you can cover with some old newspaper. Wear old clothes for painting or wear an old shirt to protect your clothes.
- Electrical tape (called insulation tape) works very nicely because it is a bit stretchy and makes a smooth edge around the top of the cans.
- You can use any decoration tape or stickers to add a magical effect.
- You may encounter some difficult steps, so make sure you have an adult close by to ask for help.

MAKING THE TRICK:

STEP 1

Cut the bottoms out of the two bigger cans using a can opener. Ask a grownup for help if you are finding this hard to do. Make sure there are no sharp edges once the bottoms are removed. DO NOT remove the bottom of the little can.

STEP 2

Painting time! Make sure you have covered your work area with old newspaper.

It's time to paint *only the insides* of the two bigger cans with black paint.

Paint the smallest can on *both the inside and outside*.

The small can is the **gimmick** that won't be seen by the audience. Leave the cans to dry.

> ### *Tips:*
> Stand the cans upright so that the paint can run down the sides and dry quicker. Leave the small can standing upside down to stop the paint collecting in the bottom, which will take a lot longer to dry.

STEP 3

Once your cans are dry, it is time to decorate your Mystery Tube. Cut some colored paper to fit around your two bigger cans. We used two different colors for the two cans so it is clearer for the audience. Decorate the cans with stickers and decorative tape. Finish off the top and bottom edges of the cans by sticking a length of electrical tape around it.

Leave the small black can undecorated. This is the most important part of creating the illusion for the Mystery Tube magic trick.

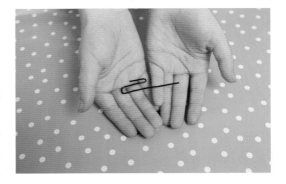

Make the "hook" for the **gimmick** by bending a paper clip into a hook or an "s" shape as shown in the pictures. This will hide the sneaky move from your audience.

STEP 4

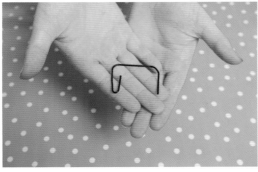

STEP 5

Cut a piece of the paper clip off with pliers. You can ask a grownup for help with this bit. You want to create a hook that looks similar to the one in the picture.

STEP 6

Stick a small piece of gaffer tape (or a similar strong tape) to the paper clip as shown.

STEP 7

Stick the paper clip hook into the small can so that it just sticks over the side. Now when you put the small can inside the other cans, it will hook onto the side while remaining hidden from the audience.

Well done!

You have made the props for your **Mystery Tube**.

Have fun producing all sorts of amazing things out of two empty cans!

HOW THE TRICK IS PERFORMED:

STEP 1

Before the performance: You have three cans for this magic trick: one large can, one medium can, and one small can. The two large cans will be decorated, with both bottoms removed. The small can should be painted black with a bottom and no decorations.

Fill the small can with colored ribbons, magician's scarves, or whatever magical item you want to pull out of the mystery tube. Place the small can into the medium can, making sure that the hook is poking over the edge. You are ready to begin the show.

STEP 2

Show the audience the big can so they can see that it is empty.

Then, slip the medium can through the large can and out again on the other side. The small can that has been placed inside the medium can will hook onto the large can, thanks to the handy paper clip hook attached to it—so now the small can is attached to the large can. Show the audience that the medium can is empty.

Insert the medium can back into the large can from the *bottom*. If you insert it from the top, the small can will be in the way since it's already hooked to the large can. Don't make the mistake of putting the can inside from the top, or your trick will be shown!

STEP 3

Moment of magic: Grab the colored ribbons or magician's scarves from the small can and pull them out from the mystery tube with a flourish, astonishing your audience who thought that the mystery tube was empty!

Rubber Band ★

Inspired by Harry Houdini, one of the most renowned magicians in history, this Rubber Band magic trick is one that will stun your audience in seconds! Houdini was famous for being an escapist—he was able to escape from seemingly impossible situations. You'll be your own Houdini with this fun trick.

Watch the Rubber Band magic trick in action using this QR code.
Or, visit the website: http://magictricksforkids.org/eb/

EFFECT (WHAT THE AUDIENCE SEES):

You have two rubber bands. One is tied around your middle finger and index finger on one hand. The other band is tied around the top parts of all four fingers. This way, the rubber band tying your middle and index fingers together can't escape. Or so your audience thinks!

Then, you do the impossible. With a flick of your fingers, the band tying your middle and index fingers together jumps to the ring and pinky finger. It is quick, simple magic that will make your audience wonder if Houdini came back from the dead and taught you this incredible trick!

YOU WILL NEED:

- 2 rubber bands (different colors)

Wrap a colored rubber band (in this case, red) twice around the base of your forefinger and middle finger. The first picture, with your palm facing downward, shows what your audience will be seeing. The second picture, with your palm facing upward, shows what is happening that is hidden from your audience's view.

HOW THE TRICK IS PERFORMED:

STEP 1

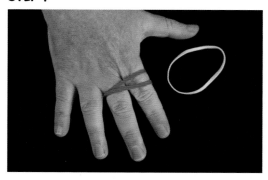

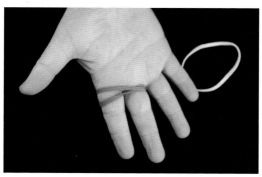

> ***Tips:***
> Using two differently colored rubber bands makes the trick more effective, and the audience can't say you are swapping the bands.

Perform this trick in front of an audience with your palm facing downward. For the purposes of this magic trick instruction, the photos here will show your palm facing upward so that you can see what is happening to the rubber band "behind the scenes."

STEP 2

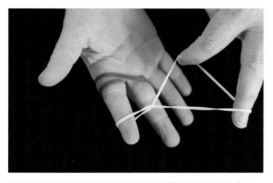

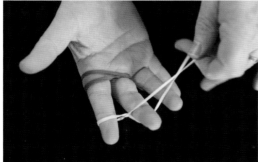

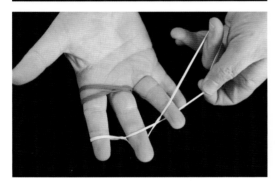

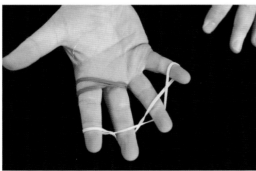

Weave the second rubber band (in this case, yellow) around the tips of all four of your fingers except

for the thumb, twisting the band after each finger. Explain to the audience that you are "locking" the red band in place so that there is no way it can move or escape. It is trapped—locked in place.

The first four pictures show what is happening under your hand, out of view from the audience. The last picture shows what your audience will see.

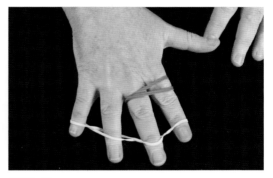

STEP 3

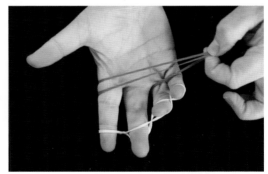

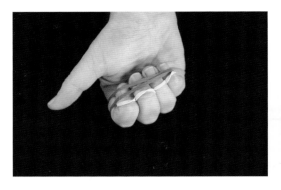

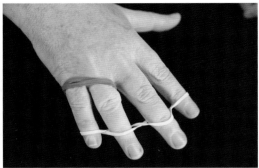

STEP 4

Sneaky move: Take the red rubber band that is wrapped around the base of your forefinger and middle finger and stretch it so that it wraps around the tips of *all* your fingers, as shown.

Speed is key here—you have to perform this move in a swift motion.

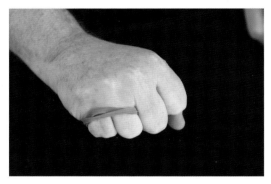

The last picture, with your palm facing downward, shows what the audience sees.

Moment of magic: Stretch out your fingers quickly from closed fist to outstretched fingers, then back to closed fist. As you open your hand, the red band will miraculously jump from the base of your forefinger and middle finger to the base of your ring and little finger. How cool is that?!

Well done!
The Rubber Band trick is really good fun and can be performed anywhere as long as you have rubber bands.

You're now your own awesome Houdini magician.

Rubber Band and Ring ★

The Rubber Band and Ring magic trick defies the earth's laws of gravity! All you need is a rubber band and a lady's ring.

Watch the video for the Rubber Band and Ring trick using this QR code.
Or, visit the website: http://magictricksforkids.org/rmt/

EFFECT (WHAT THE AUDIENCE SEES):

You place a ring through a cut rubber band that you hold between your two hands. You tilt the rubber band at an angle and the audience watches the ring move down the slope.

Then, the real magic happens. Using your magician's mind power, you are able to move the ring up the slope! Everyone's eyes will be glued to that ring as it defies gravity!

YOU WILL NEED:

- Ring
- Rubber band (do not use a thick, flat rubber band)
- Scissors

> *Tips:*
> Although this simple trick is very easy to perform, you will have to work harder on the presentation of the trick than on the actual doing of the trick.

MAKING THE TRICK:

STEP 1

Cut a rubber band so you can stretch it into a straight line. You're ready to begin!

HOW THE TRICK IS PERFORMED:

STEP 1

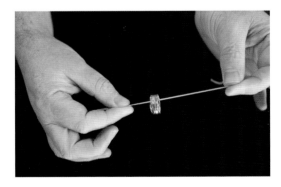

Borrow a ring from an audience member. A thinnish, narrow, and round (not flat) ring works best. Assure them that you won't do anything to damage their ring.

STEP 2

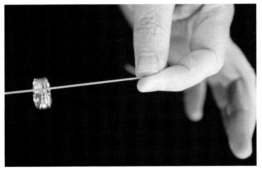

Slip the rubber band through the ring. Pinch the ends of the rubber band between your forefinger and thumb on both hands and stretch until taut.

Sneaky move: When you pinch the rubber band with your forefinger and thumb, grab it slightly away from the very end, leaving an extra bit of rubber band hanging behind your fingers. Make sure your hands are covering these extra bits so the audience can't see them.

STEP 3

Tilt the rubber band at an angle, with your left hand elevated and your right hand below, and with the ring at the top of the slope.

Let the ring slide down to your right hand.

STEP 4

Moment of magic: Here's how you defy gravity: While still holding your rubber band stretched and taut, gradually and gently release the pressure on your right hand. As you release your hold on the rubber band, it will slip through your fingers, and, as it does, the ring will appear to move upward.

Although it looks like the ring is moving up the rubber band, what's really happening is that the ring is simply staying on the same spot of the band. When the tension in the band is released, the elastic shrinks back to it's original size, creating an illusion of the ring moving upward, defying all laws of gravity!

STEP 5

As this is such a simple magic trick to do, work on your presentation to mystify and entertain your audience.

I've added a "blow" on the ring as it moves upward to add some flair!

Well done!
You can now do this simple magic trick.
Have fun!

Rope ★

Magicians have special tools that they always carry with them. One of these is the magician's silk handkerchief. These soft, thin pieces of cloth are important to every magic show. In the Rope magic trick, you'll be using the magician's handkerchief and a piece of rope to wow your audience.

> Watch the demonstration and tutorial video for the Rope magic trick using this QR code.
> Or, visit the website: http://magictricksforkids.org/ropemt/

EFFECT (WHAT THE AUDIENCE SEES):

You have a magician's handkerchief and a long cotton rope on the table. You show the audience how you keep your precious magician's handkerchiefs in one place by tying them onto a cotton rope loop so they can't be easily stolen.

You then ask your audience if they want to see how you easily remove the handkerchiefs when you need them for your magic show. With a single tug on the cloth, you magically pull it apart from the cotton rope without untying it!

YOU WILL NEED:

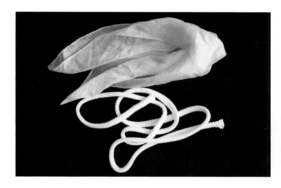

- Thick cotton rope or string (about 40 inches)
- Silk handkerchief

> ## Tips:
> In the Rope magic trick, you will make a silk handkerchief pass right through a piece of rope or string, in front of your audience's eyes. This magic effect is called a **penetration**.

HOW THE TRICK IS PERFORMED:

STEP 1
Show the audience your rope and silk handkerchief. Tell them the significance of your handkerchiefs and how they're very special to you as a superstar magician. Explain that whenever you're not doing a show, you tie your handkerchiefs securely to a rope in order to keep them in one place and ensure that they do not get stolen.

STEP 2

Fold the length of rope in half.

STEP 3

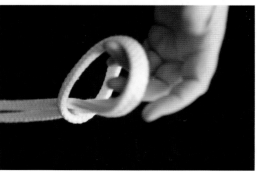

Now, fold the rope over itself to create a loop as shown. Pick the rope up by pinching the two parallel lengths of rope together as shown.

Now, thread these two long ropes through the loop by pulling them through the hole. This creates another loop at the end.

STEP 5

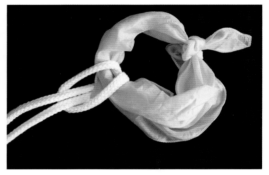

Then, tell the audience that to be doubly sure your handkerchief doesn't get stolen, you are going to tie another knot.

Tie the ends of the silk together with a double knot. It appears that you have now tied the silk securely onto the rope such that it cannot be removed easily.

STEP 4

Insert the hankie through the loop and pull the rope tight onto the silk. It looks like you have now tied the rope onto the silk.

Explain to the audience that you're tying it tight so no one can steal your precious handkerchief.

STEP 6

ends of the rope tightly is that the rope will be pulled over the handkerchief and the rope's knot will become undone. However, the handkerchief will still seem to be tied to the rope.

STEP 7

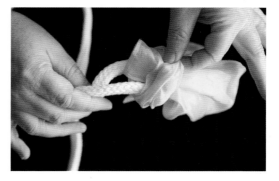

Now, explain to the audience that as the great magician you are, in cases of emergency you can remove the handkerchief quickly if you need to with your amazing skills.

Moment of magic: Grab hold of the handkerchief, as shown, and give it a tug. The handkerchief will magically come off the rope! You can even ask an audience member to pull on the handkerchief to make it more believable.

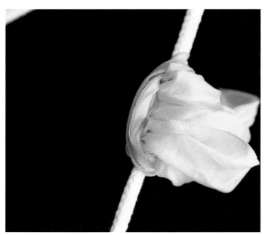

Grab hold of a piece of rope in each hand and pull the rope tightly to secure. Now no one could ever steal it!

Sneaky move: What's actually happening when you pull the

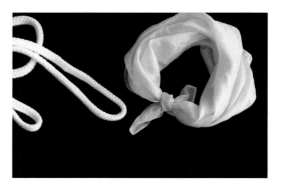

Signed Card to Wallet ★

The Signed Card to Wallet magic trick is a mind-boggling performance that will get your audience on their feet to applaud the superstar magician—you! Similar magic trick kits can be found at your local magic shops, but this trick is much simpler to do.

You can watch the video for the Signed Card to Wallet trick here using this QR code.
Or, visit the website: http://magictricksforkids.org/sctw/

EFFECT (WHAT THE AUDIENCE SEES):

You ask an audience member to pick a card from a deck of cards and sign it on the face side. You separate the card deck in half and place the audience member's card in the center of the deck.

You shuffle the cards and place the deck on the table. You flip the deck over and fan through the cards to show your volunteer that you've made the card magically disappear from the center of the deck.

You then pull out your wallet to reveal a face down card. You remove the card from your wallet, place it on top of the card deck, then flip the top card over and show your audience that it's the signed card! Your crowd will explode with applause for you and your incredible talents!

YOU WILL NEED:

- Wallet
- Pack of cards
- Felt tip marker pen
- Magician's wax
- Double-backed card (page 15, **step 1**)

> ### Tips:
> To do this trick you need something called **magician's wax**. You can get this wax from magic shops or from online shops on the Internet.
>
> The second secret item you need is a **double-backed card**. This is a card that has the back of a card printed on both sides.
>
> You can make a double-backed card by sticking two cards together face-to-face (page 15, **step 1**).

MAKING THE TRICK:

STEP 1

Take a small piece of magician's wax and make a small ball.

> ### Tip:
> 100% beeswax will also work in place of magician's wax.

STEP 2

Stick the small ball of wax on one side of the double-backed card.

STEP 3

Place the double-backed card in the wallet with the wax on the side that's facing down.

> ### Well done!
> You are now ready to perform the Signed Card to Wallet magic trick!

HOW THE TRICK IS PERFORMED:

STEP 1

Ask an audience member to choose a card from your deck without showing it to you. Have them sign the face of the card.

STEP 2

Next, cut the deck of cards in half to create two piles. Tell the audience member to place their signed card on top of one of the piles, then replace the other pile back on top. It now looks like the signed card is in the center of the deck.

STEP 3

Sneaky move: You will be using a card control technique, called the "injog," to secretly place the signed card back on top of the deck.

In **step 2**, when you replace the other pile back on top of the signed card, slip the top card of that pile onto the signed card, but place it halfway, with an edge jutting out off the signed card. This is how you mark the location of the signed card.

Then, pretend to shuffle the deck to mix up the cards, but what you're really doing is shuffling only the top half of the deck that is above the signed card. Make your shuffling messy so that the audience won't see the first card that is jutting out and marking the location of the signed card.

When you've finished shuffling, grab the top half pile by putting your fingers under the first card that is jutting out, and move the pile underneath the rest of the card deck. The signed card is now on the top of the deck.

> ### Tip:
> Here is a video lesson that will teach you how to perform the injog card control technique: https://www.youtube.com/watch?v=2wBDDKZCNy0

STEP 4

Wave your fingers over the deck and tell the audience that you have made their selected card magically disappear from the deck. Turn the cards over to reveal the card faces and slowly fan out the deck to show that the signed card is nowhere to be seen; however, stop short of showing them the very last card in the deck, as this is where the signed card is.

Turn the deck over so the cards are face down again and the signed card is back on top.

STEP 5

Next, take out your wallet from your pocket and remove the double-back card without revealing the other side with the wax stuck on it. Place the card, wax-side down, on top of the deck and discreetly press on top of it so that the wax sticks to the signed card.

Flip the card over and reveal the signed card, which the audience thinks you have just removed from your wallet!

Spoon-Bending Illusion ★

Do you want to make dinnertime even more exciting and fun? You may not be able to play with your food, but there's no rule that you can't play with spoons, right? Try the Spoon-Bending Illusion magic trick and shock your family and friends.

> See a video of the Spoon-Bending Illusion trick using this QR code.
> Or, visit the website: http://magictricksforkids.org/sb/

EFFECT (WHAT THE AUDIENCE SEES):

You have a spoon in your hand. You push down on the spoon and it bends! Then, you flip the spoon in your hands and "go back in time," revealing the original state of the spoon before you bent it! Whether you do this in a restaurant or at a dinner table, all eyes will be on the spoon you're magically bending.

YOU WILL NEED:

- Dessert spoon
- Table

Tips:

The spoon-bending illusion was made famous by Uri Geller back in the 1970s.

This version uses no special props and you'll be able to perform it in minutes.

The illusion is done by holding the spoon in a special way. You need to pay attention to your angles when performing this illusion.

HOW THE TRICK IS PERFORMED:

The illusion works when you have the perfect grip on your spoon, holding it only with your little finger. However, to the audience, it looks like you've wrapped both hands around the spoon.

Start by holding the spoon as shown in the picture, with your little finger gripping the part of the handle that is closest to the head of the spoon. The front view of the spoon is what your audience sees.

STEP 1

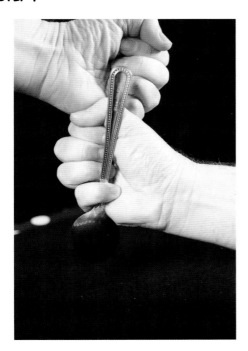

STEP 2

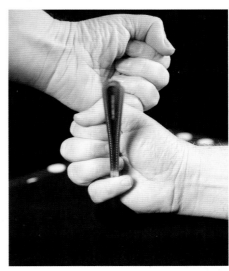

Sneaky move: Now, slowly release the grip around the handle by opening your little finger slightly while your fists pretend to push down on the table, as if you are bending the spoon with the force of your hands.

STEP 3

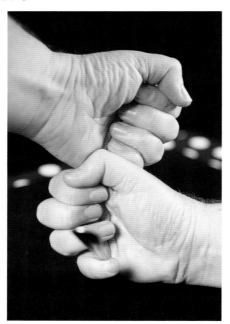

Continue releasing the grip to complete the illusion, making it appear that the spoon has been bent completely.

STEP 4

Complete the illusion by gripping the spoon with your little finger again to bring the handle back up to the starting position, so the spoon appears to magically unbend. Turn the spoon over and lie it on the table for inspection.

Well done!

You have learned how to perform the amazing **Spoon-Bending Illusion**.

Have fun with this mentalism effect.

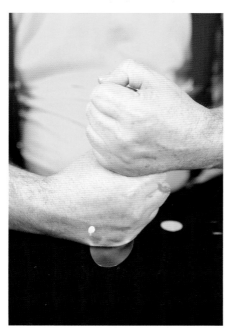

Square Circle ★

Have you ever seen magicians make things appear out of thin air and wonder how on earth they managed to do the impossible? You won't be puzzling anymore when you learn to pull a string of colorful scarves (and an extra treat) out from nowhere!

See how the Square Circle trick is performed in this video using this QR code.
Or, visit the website: http://magictricksforkids.org/sc/

EFFECT (WHAT THE AUDIENCE SEES):

You have a box with a window grill on the front side to show your audience that there's nothing inside. However, when you lift up the box, you pull out a long string of colorful scarves, amazing your audience.

YOU WILL NEED:

- 4 pieces of A4- or letter-sized thick colored card or a square box (See the **Tips** section)
- Set of nesting tins (2) or 2 different-sized food tins (see the **Tips** section)
- Scissors
- Chalkboard paint (black)
- Paintbrush (1 or 1.5 inch)
- Decorative tape, stickers, buttons, beads etc.
- See-through sticky tape
- Can opener
- Newspaper and an old shirt
- Magician's scarves or anything else you want to reveal to your audience

Tips:

For the square: Use thick card paper as it works really well and keeps the shape of the square nicely. Or, you could use square-shaped cardboard by cutting the top and bottom flappy bits off a cardboard box.

Recommended measurements:
- Four squares measuring 8 x 8 inches each.

For the tins: A nesting set of tins works really well (biscuit tins or coffee/sugar/tea tins that fit into one another). They are normally sold in sets of three and you can get them from your local grocery store in the home or kitchen aisles. If you can't find these, tinned food cans will work.

Recommended measurements:
- Smaller tin: diameter of up to 4 inches, height 4.5 inches.
- Larger tin: diameter of from 4.5 to 6 inches, height 6 inches.

We are going to be painting to make this trick (yeah!). You will need an area that you can cover with old newspaper so you don't dirty anything. It is also a good idea to wear old clothes.

There are some tricky bits that you may need help with, so make sure you have a grown-up nearby.

MAKING THE TRICK:

STEP 1

Cut out four pieces of thick cardboard measuring 8 x 8 inches each. Paint the backs of all the squares with black chalkboard paint. If you are using a box, paint the inside of the box with the chalkboard paint. Be careful not to get paint on the presentation side (the side that the audience will see). Leave to dry.

STEP 2

Using the can opener, remove the bottom of the *big* can only, so you are left with a hollow tube. Make sure there are no sharp edges along the sides.

STEP 3

Paint the inside of the *big* tin only with black chalkboard paint. You may need to do a few coats of paint to get an even cover.

STEP 4

Now paint the inside and the outside of the *smaller* tin. This is your load chamber (the sneaky move) and it will not be seen by your audience. Paint a few coats to cover it evenly. Leave your tins to dry.

> ### *Tip:*
> It is helpful to stand the smaller tin upside down so that the paint doesn't collect at the bottom, which may take a lot longer to dry.

STEP 5

Your squares (or box) should be dry by now. Measure and cut out a grid of diagonal lines in one of the squares (or one of the sides of the box) as shown in the picture. This will be the "window" grills on your box.

By cutting these diagonal lines, it adds to the **misdirection** in the performance, as it makes it almost impossible to see the vertical sides of the can when it is placed inside the square.

STEP 6

Decorate the grills on the square (or the side on the box). We used stickers and decorative tape, but you can add buttons, beads, and any other decorations you want. Remember, this is what your audience will be seeing when you are performing this effect.

If you used a box, you can skip steps 7–8.

STEP 7

Stick the last two sides together, from the inside. The black painted sides should be facing inward. Add some decorative tape along the sides of the square to give it a neat finish. This helps to strengthen your box.

Now, we are going to combine the four squares into a box. Place the four squares (with the black painted sides facing up) next to the another. Stick the sides of two squares together with see-through sticky tape. Stick the side of the third square to the first two squares. Now stick the last square to your row of squares. All your squares should be attached in a row.

STEP 8

Well done!
Now you have your props for one of the most amazing tricks you can do.

HOW THE TRICK IS PERFORMED:

STEP 1

Before the performance: Put the magician's scarves into the smaller black tin. You should place a black scarf at the very top so that the vibrantly colored scarves will not accidentally flash and reveal themselves to the audience. You can even place a fun item at the bottom of the can, such as a stuffed animal or a rubber ball that you can toss around. This tin will be hiding throughout the show and the audience should not see it.

Place the smaller tin in the square box, and place the bigger tin over the smaller tin. The grills on the side of the square box should be facing your audience. You are ready to begin.

STEP 2

In front of the audience, remove the bigger tin from the square box and show them that it is hollow and doesn't have a bottom.

The audience will also be able to see through the window grills of the box and notice that the inside of the box is "empty." However, they won't realize that the smaller tin, your loading chamber that holds the magician's scarves, is actually disguised inside the box, its black surface blending into the box's black interior.

STEP 3

Put the bigger tin back into the box, secretly placing it over the smaller tin. Now, lift the square and show the audience that it is also hollow with nothing inside. The key is to make sure you don't reveal the small painted tin. Place the square back over the tin.

STEP 4

Flourish your magic wand and pull out the colorful magician's scarves from the small tin! You have become a magician who can pull anything out of thin air (or, from well-disguised tin cans)! Your audience will be completely fooled.

Strength Tester Optical Illusion ★

An optical illusion is another word for a visual illusion. It's like an object that is playing magic tricks on you when you perceive the images of it differently. As the great magician you are, you'll be playing visual tricks on your audience with this super duper easy optical illusion.

Watch a short video demonstration of the Strength Tester Optical Illusion trick using this QR code.

Or, visit the website: http://magictricksforkids. org/oi/

EFFECT (WHAT THE AUDIENCE SEES):

You are going to test your strength against an assistant or an audience member.

You hold two curved pieces of paper in front of you that look about the same size to your audience. Your assistant takes one of the pieces, and both of you test your strength by pulling on the piece as hard as you can using both hands. Take the piece back from your assistant, hold it up beside yours, and watch your audience be shocked and mystified because the pieces are now somehow drastically different in size.

YOU WILL NEED:

- Scissors
- "Strength Tester" printout (page 121)
- Stickers and decorative tape

MAKING THE TRICK:

STEP 1

Print the "Strength Tester" printout on cardboard and cut out the curved pieces. You can also print it on paper, cut it out, and stick it onto some card so it is sturdy.

STEP 2

If you want, you can decorate your curved pieces with stickers, decorative tape, and felt tips. You can even trace the two shapes onto different colored or patterned cardboard if you don't like the pattern and color on our printout.

Have fun with decorating—make it look magical!

HOW THE TRICK IS PERFORMED:

STEP 1

You have two curved pieces. Hold up the pieces in front of you so your audience can see that they are similar in size.

Let your assistant take one of the pieces—the one that seems a bit longer than the other one.

STEP 2

Both of you pretend to pull on the pieces as hard as you can to test your strength for a few seconds.

Sneaky move: Take your assistant's piece with your right hand and hold the pieces upright in front of the audience, side-by-side. However, position your right hand slightly further in front of you than your left hand. To the audience, your assistant's piece now looks a lot longer than your piece!

Well done!

Optical illusions are great fun and the Strength Tester is a real hit.

The beauty of this optical illusion is you can do it again and again; it is always effective.

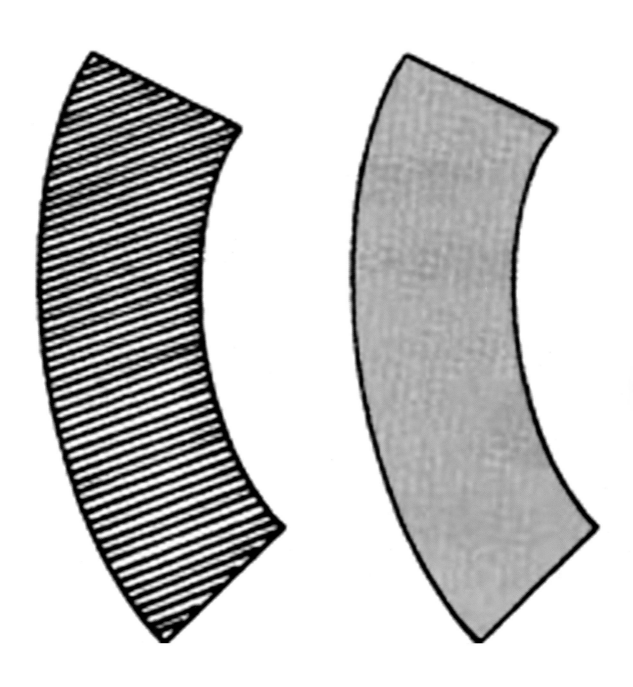

Sticky Magic Wand ★

When it comes to magic tricks with wands, this is probably the easiest. You can perform the Sticky Magic Wand trick right after the Growing Magic Wand trick (page 47).

EFFECT (WHAT THE AUDIENCE SEES):

This wand magically "sticks" to your opened hand . . . and then drops on your command!

YOU WILL NEED:

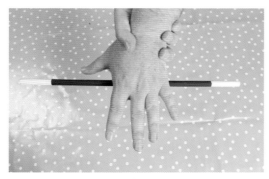

- Magic Wand (page 49–50, **steps 1–2**)

HOW THE TRICK IS PERFORMED:

STEP 1

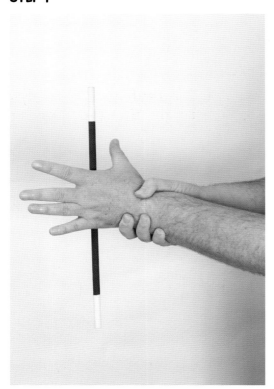

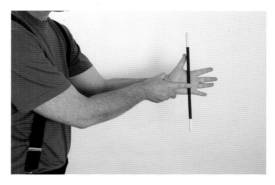

Create the illusion of the wand "sticking" to your hand by keeping it in place with your index finger, which is hidden by your other hand.

STEP 2
To drop it, simply lift your finger! Remember to watch your **angles**.

Well done!
Have fun amazing everyone with this simplest of magic tricks!

Telekinesis Pen Levitation ★

You don't need gravity for this trick! Levitating is one of the most popular magic tricks you can perform, and you will make a pen dance inside a glass bottle without any support (or so the audience thinks!). This telekinesis pen levitation trick is serious stuff, but still really easy to do.

Check out the video for the Telekinesis Pen Levitation trick using this QR code.

Or, visit the website: http://magictricks-forkids.org/tpl/

EFFECT (WHAT THE AUDIENCE SEES):

You slide a pen inside a glass bottle, which is then placed on its side. With a wave of your magic wand or a snap of your fingers, you slowly tilt the bottle upward.

   With your powerful magical skills, you swirl the bottle gently in your hand. The pen will slowly move up and down, poking its head outside the bottle rim. You've just defied the basic laws of gravity!

YOU WILL NEED:

- Ball point pen
- Glass bottle
- Invisible thread
- Safety pin
- See-through sticky tape
- Scissors

> ### *Tips:*
>
> Invisible thread, the **gimmick**, is the secret to this trick. You can find invisible thread online by searching on the Internet. Working with invisible thread requires a bit of patience as it is very fine and hard to see (but that is the whole point, remember!).
>
> Once you've mastered the technique of making the pen move and lift (seemingly with the powers of your mind), work on your presentation. This trick is enhanced by a really good performance.

MAKING THE TRICK:

STEP 1

You need the thread to be long enough to extend from your chest to your hand when holding the bottle outstretched in front of you—about an arm's length.

Remove the ink chamber of the ballpoint pen from the plastic tube as shown. Wrap the end of a piece of invisible thread around the pen tip.

(For the purpose of these instructions, I have used black cotton thread so you can see what to do with your invisible thread in these pictures.)

STEP 2

Secure the thread around the tip of the pen with a small piece of see-through sticky tape. Don't use too much, or else it will prevent the ink chamber from sliding back into the plastic tube, and you want the pen to look un-gimmicked. Push the ink chamber back into the tube, now with the invisible thread tied around it.

STEP 3

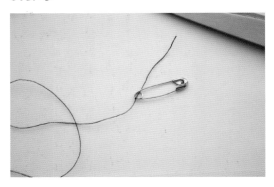

Tie the other end of the invisible thread to a safety pin. This takes lots of patience, so take your time!

STEP 4

Attach the safety pin to the underside of your clothing and make sure it is hidden from view.

Well done!
You are ready to perform the Telekinesis Pen Levitation trick!

HOW THE TRICK IS PERFORMED:

STEP 1

In front of your audience, place the pen, tip point down, into the bottle.

The thread now runs from the pen over the rim of the bottle to the hidden safety pin attached under your clothes. Be careful with your movements as the thread might snap if it gets caught by accident.

STEP 2

Move the bottle closer and further away from yourself, or rotate it slowly. The tension on the invisible thread will pull on the pen, making it levitate and rise out of the bottle as if powered by your mind! To add to your performance, wave your hands or snap your fingers as you levitate the pen.

You can even give an audience member the glass bottle and pen after secretly breaking the invisible thread, telling them to check and investigate the items. They'll be so impressed by your magical mind powers that they'll be asking you, "How'd you do it?!"

Unlinking Drinking Straws ★

You love sipping your favorite juice through straws, right? But what if I told you you can use those same straws to perform an illusion-tastic magic trick where a solid object will pass through another object? The Unlinking Drinking Straw trick is so simple and will take you just a few minutes to learn.

Watch the video for the Unlinking Drinking Straws trick using this QR code.
Or, visit the website: http://magictricksforkids.org/uds/

EFFECT (WHAT THE AUDIENCE SEES):

You have two straws that you tie together in a knot. You grab the ends of the straws and show the knot to your audience. Then, you magically pull the straws apart and the straws go through each other!

YOU WILL NEED:

- 2 plastic drinking straws (preferably different colors)

Tips:

Doing magic with everyday objects is good fun—this is called **impromptu magic**. The next time you are out at a restaurant, you can easily perform this trick!

The secret to this trick is in how you wrap the straws around one another. Pay careful attention to the instructions, practice often, and have fun!

HOW THE TRICK IS PERFORMED

STEP 1

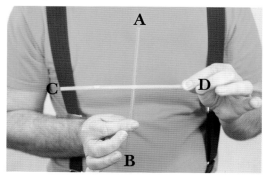

Hold the pink straw in your right hand vertically (|) (**AB**). Place it behind the yellow straw in your left hand, which you are holding in a horizontal position (—) (**CD**). The straws should make a cross.

STEP 2

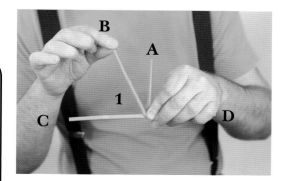

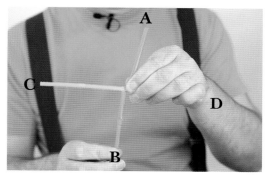

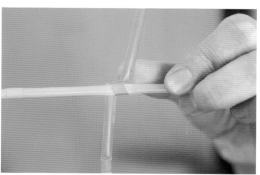

Wrap the vertical pink straw (**AB**) around the horizontal yellow straw (**CD**) as shown. Make sure that the straw passes through the top left quarter (**1**) of the cross, then pull it downward to wrap it around.

STEP 3

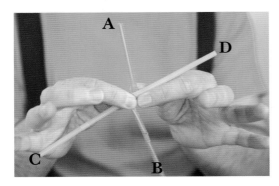

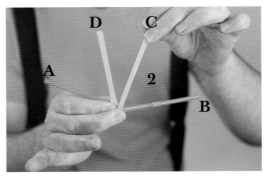

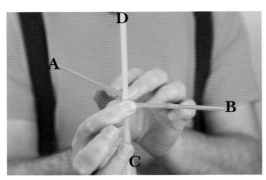

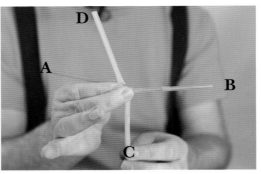

Turn the straws clockwise (from your perspective) so that the pink straw (**AB**) is now horizontal and the yellow straw (**CD**) is now vertical. The pictures show what your audience will be seeing.

Now wrap the vertical yellow straw (**CD**) around the horizontal pink straw (**AB**) from the front to the back as shown. Make sure that the yellow straw passes through the top right quarter (**2**) of the cross.

STEP 4

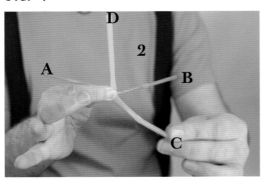

STEP 5

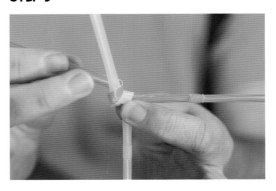

You will now have a "knot."

STEP 6

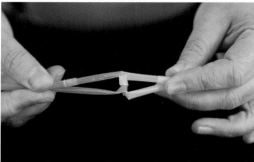

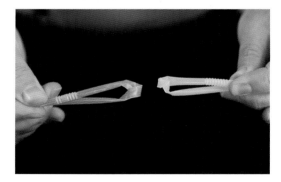

Moment of magic: bring the ends of the pink straw and yellow straw together and give a gentle pull. Your straws should now separate as if by magic!

Show the audience that the straws did not break and are intact. You have successfully passed one solid straw through another!

Well done!
Have fun with this impromptu magic trick!

Vanishing Matchbox ★

Don't worry, you won't be creating fires or doing anything dangerous with these matches. You'll only need a matchbox for this simple but awesome magic trick that will light a fire of curiosity and mystery for your audience!

Check out the video for the Vanishing Matchbox magic trick using this QR code.
Or, visit the website: http://magictricksforkids.org/vm/

EFFECT (WHAT THE AUDIENCE SEES):

You show the audience an empty matchbox in your hand. You wrap your hand around the matchbox, turn your hand over, and push the matchbox's sliding component out of your hand.

When you open your hand, the outside cover of the matchbox has vanished into thin air and has instead been magically transferred to the inside of your hat! You will be known as the great magician who can make anything disappear!

YOU WILL NEED:

- Scissors
- Two matchboxes
- Glue stick
- Hat

> ### *Tips:*
> With this trick, you will be learning the basic principle of **sleight of hand**, which is a method of close-up magic used by many magicians.
> You won't need the matches, just the two empty matchboxes.

MAKING THE TRICK:

STEP 1

Empty the matchboxes. You can throw the matches away or keep them somewhere safe for future use.

STEP 2

Now, you will be using only one of the matchboxes. Remove the empty tray and work on the cover sleeve.

Cut along the side of the matchbox's sleeve so that it opens up.

STEP 3

Cut off the bottom rectangle of the matchbox sleeve as shown. You won't be using this.

STEP 4

Cut one of the "lighting" sides off; you also won't be using this. You will be left with the top part of the matchbox sleeve, one side of the lighting sides, and the empty tray that the matches were in.

STEP 5

Spread glue on the back of the matchbox sleeve. Cover the bottom and one side of the tray with glue.

STEP 6

Stick the matchbox sleeve onto the tray as shown.

STEP 7

Trim off the edges of the sleeve if they are sticking over the sides of the tray.

Well done!
You have made your **gimmick**, which will be the main part of your magic trick! It is in fact an empty matchbox tray that has a matchbox sleeve cover design glued to its underside. When you flip it over, it will look like a complete matchbox with a cover sleeve over a tray.

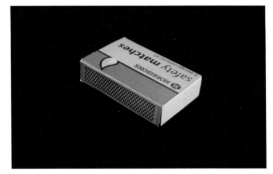

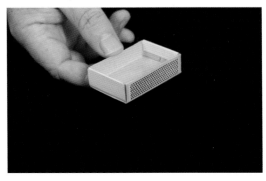

HOW THE TRICK IS PERFORMED

STEP 1

Before the performance: You have the **gimmick** (the empty tray with the matchbox sleeve design glued to the back) and an extra matchbox. Remove the cover sleeve from the extra matchbox and place it in the hat on your head. It will stay there throughout the performance until the end!

STEP 2

In front of your audience, hold up the gimmicked matchbox in one hand, bottom-side up, so they see the cover design glued onto the empty matchbox.

Be careful about your presentation to fool your audience into thinking this is a whole matchbox! Make sure you're not revealing the empty tray on the bottom.

STEP 3

Sneaky move: quickly place your other hand over the matchbox, secretly rolling it over onto its bottom side while it hides under your hand. You will now hold the matchbox with this hand, palm facing downward.

STEP 4

With your other hand, extend an index finger and push the matchbox out of your hand. The audience will see the empty tray coming out.

STEP 5

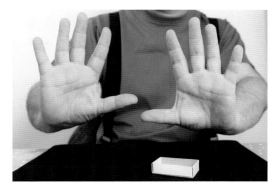

Moment of magic: Open your hand to reveal that you've made the matchbox sleeve disappear. Wait as your audience applauds you.

STEP 6

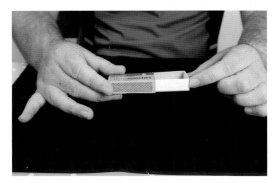

Then, lift up your hat and let the other matchbox cover fall out. You'll get a second round of applause for not only making the matchbox sleeve vanish but also appearing magically in your hat!

To end the performance, you can slip the empty tray back into the matchbox sleeve. Ta-da!

Well done!

Remember to practice this trick to perfect your sleight of hand technique.

Afterword ★

This is the last page of this book, but I hope it's not the end. It is my wish that you take the magic tricks you have learned here, practice them, and show them to your friends and family. If you do that then this is not the end but rather the beginning.

Let me tell you one final story.

There was once a young boy who found a magic book just like the one you now hold in your hands.

The young boy read the tricks and practiced the routines in front of a mirror. He showed his family his new magic skills and they were amazed and proud. The young boy performed magic for his friends, and he quickly became popular at school.

The young boy continued to read other books on magic, and he performed regularly for pocket money. At the age of sixteen, he was invited to his first television appearance.

The young boy grew into a man who made his living doing magic. He traveled the world entertaining people and doing what he loved. He appeared on television many times and was featured in the newspaper dozens of times. The local people from his hometown recognized him and knew his name whenever he walked down the street. One day, thanks to a newspaper appearance, he found the love of his life and they got married—all thanks to magic.

The young boy was now a married man, and he decided to focus his attention on teaching magic to children who wanted to learn the art. One day, he received an email asking him if he wanted to write a book about magic and, with the help of his daughter and wife, he did.

You now hold that book in your hands. That little boy was me.

Looking back all those years ago when I read my very first magic book, I had no idea where this journey would lead me.

It's now your turn.

You are now a young child with a magic book.

So, as you can see, this is not the end; this is the beginning.

This is the beginning to your story.

Thanks for being part of my journey.

—Ken Kelly and the Kelly family